Mary E Kail

Crown Our Heroes

And Other Poems

Mary E Kail

Crown Our Heroes
And Other Poems

ISBN/EAN: 9783744705288

Printed in Europe, USA, Canada, Australia, Japan

Cover: Foto ©Thomas Meinert / pixelio.de

More available books at **www.hansebooks.com**

CROWN OUR HEROES

AND

OTHER POEMS.

BY

MRS. MARY E. KAIL.

---

*This book is offered, that this book may be
A friend to you, as it has been to me ;
For through the trials of the passing years,
To write its lines was balm for all my tears.*

WASHINGTON, D. C. :
JUDD & DETWEILER, PRINTERS.
1887.

TO

THE GRAND ARMY OF THE REPUBLIC;

EVERY LIVING AND EVERY DEAD SOLDIER;

AND TO

MRS. LELAND STANFORD,

WHOSE GENTLE CHRISTIAN SYMPATHY HAS SOOTHED

SO MANY SUFFERING HEARTS, AND BROUGHT

THE

MORNING OF JOY

TO THE HOME OF THE AUTHOR.

CONTENTS.

	PAGE.
Crown Our Heroes	1
General Grant's Funeral Ode	2
To Mrs. Leland Stanford	4
Poem of Welcome	6
Thou Hast Won My Heart to Love Thee	7
Flowers Around the Picture	8
A Spray of Jasmine	10
We Sing of the Merry Harvest-Time	11
Little Effie	12
Some One	13
How We Journey	14
A Picture of Life	15
Two Natures	17
Blue Morning-Glory	18
Genius	19
Two Altars	20
A Shower of Roses	21
An Autumn Day	22
Rest, Mother, Rest	24
Sweet Vale of Connotton	25
Crocus	27
If we Could Know	28
Jonquil	30
Pretty Little Maiden	31
Our Silver Wedding Song	32
Morning, Noon, and Night	34
I Am Trusting in God	35
His Footstep at the Door	37
Daffodil	38

CONTENTS.

	PAGE.
My Little Son and I	39
We Silently Slumber at Last	40
Pretty Robin-Redbreast	41
Frozen	42
Rest	43
Autumn Glory	44
Ohio	46
Come Where the Flowers Lie Sleeping	47
For Me, Sweet Birds	49
There Is a Difference	50
Emancipation Day	51
A Winter Day	54
My Love of Long Ago	55
My Love is True to Me	56
A Reverie	57
Marguerite	59
On the Evergreen Shore	60
The Recompense of Faith	61
Rest, Noble Hero, Rest	63
What is Poetry	64
The Old Hearthstone	66
A Song of Sadness	67
Tell Me Roses	69
Summer Weather	70
Sometime	71
Sea-Anemones	72
The Voice of the Roses	74
The River's Answer	75
I Envy Not	77
Inauguration Ode	78
Beautiful Violets	80
A Fragment	81
Heaven Bless the Little Boys	82
Farewell to the Ohio Editors	83
In Silence Now	84
Centennial Ode	85
Mabel	88
Faded Lilies	89
A Gift of Roses	90

CONTENTS.

	PAGE.
A Welcome	91
At Last	95
Oh, No, Not There	99
Silvery Waves	100
At the Gate I Wait for Thee	101
Under the Roof-tree	102
Our Thanksgiving	103
From the Rill to the Ocean	104
Lines in a Young Lady's Album	106
Violets	107
Claribel Lee	108
The Pauper	109
Oh, Sing for me a Song To-night	111
By and By the Roses Wither	112
At Close of Day	113
I Was Waiting for a Letter	114
I'm Dreaming I'm an Infant	115
My Mother's Flowers	117
Tell Me, Darling, that You Miss Me	118
I'll Dream Love of Thee	119
Jennie Vernon	121
Summer Night	123
The Music of Tears	124
Send Me	125
I Am Weary, Oh, My Father	126
Softly and Low	127
To My Bride of Thirty Years	128
What Shall We Name the Baby?	129
Gloomy Weather	131
An Autumn Revery	132
Cold, My Darling	134
Give Me Back My Childhood	135
Life is Short and Death is Near	136
In the Garden	137
Into the Fields With Golden Grain	138
Bitter Wine	139
Cast Off	140
Then Life Were Worth the Living	142
Only a Woman's Smile	144

CONTENTS.

	PAGE.
Our Angel Watchers	145
Another Year	146
Thrice Wedded	147
Brightness	149
Submission	150
Departed June	151
With the Gift of a Rose	152
Gentle Words	153
Little Mary	154
Where Shall the Soul Find Rest	156
To an Old Friend	157

CROWN OUR HEROES.

CROWN OUR HEROES.

[The following poem was read by Mrs. Davidson, of Alabama, Decoration Day, 1881, at the tomb of Washington, on the occasion of the visit to that place of George Washington Post, G. A. R., Gen. M. T. McMahon, commanding, the verses placed in their archives and the writer presented with the badge of the Post, a gold hatchet on blue silk.]

Crown our heroes, the soldiers, whose spirits have fled
To the land of the blest: crown the heroic dead.
Let the fair hand of woman weave garlands of flowers
Kissed by heaven's pure sunlight in sweet morning hours.
Go tenderly, gently, and scatter them where
Our heroes are sleeping,—go scatter them there.

Crown our heroes, the soldiers, who sleep on the shore
Where the call of the bugle can wake them no more.
Men who fought to defend us—oh, can we forget
The tribute of glory we owe to them yet?
Bring love's fairest offerings, with tears and with prayer,
And gratefully, sacredly scatter them there.

Crown our heroes, the soldiers, whose grandeur and power
Saved our own dear Columbia in war's troubled hour—
When amid the fierce struggle each soul was a host,
Who was ready to die lest his country be lost.
They are dead! they are dead! what now can we do
As a token of love for the noble and true?

Crown our heroes, the soldiers. Oh ! scatter the flowers
O'er the graves of the dead : they are yours, they are ours.
Men who fought for the flag, and our foes in the fray ;
For as brothers they sleep, both the blue and the gray.
And true to our banner, our offerings we bring,—
Blushing roses of summer, and violets of spring.

Crown our heroes, God bless them ! no true heart must lag :
Crown the dead and the living who stood by the flag.
Through the oncoming ages let each have a name
Carved in letters of gold in the temple of fame ;
For the bright Stars of Freedom—our banner unfurled—
Is the joy of Columbia, the pride of the world !

GENERAL GRANT'S FUNERAL ODE.

[From Memorial Edition of the NATIONAL REPUBLICAN.]

Muffle the drums, for the hero is dead !
    And our tears tell the sorrowing story ;
From pain and from suffering his spirit has fled,
    And we bury our chief in his glory.
Nevermore shall the voice of the clarion's call
    Wake the dearly loved form from its sleeping ;
Whisper low ! let the music in reverence fall,
    While around him a nation is weeping.

Our tears for the hero while angels proclaim,
    He has passed o'er the heavenly portal,
Where wreaths of the victor and laurels of fame
    Have been changed for the glory immortal.
Rest, soldier, rest, for 'tis joyful to know—
    Ah, was it e'er known by another?—
Gallant men, who once stood in the ranks of the foe,
    Love you now as a friend and a brother.

Round his grave we will gather with tributes of love,
    And the songs of his country's devotion,
While the flag of Columbia floats proudly above,
    Reaching out to the isles of the ocean.
And 'mid glory awaiting the on-coming years,
    Loving friends shall plant summer's sweet flowers,
That shall blossom and bloom 'neath their fast falling tears
    O'er the grave of this hero of ours.

Mufflle the drums while the people draw near,
    Every heart with a voice of caressing ;
Touch gently the chords of each memory dear
    For it brings us a boon and a blessing.
Fold softly his battle flags over his breast
    And disturb not his wonderful sleeping ;
With a world's benediction our hero shall rest
    While his spirit is safe in Heaven's keeping.

TO MRS. LELAND STANFORD.

AN ANGEL CAME TO ME WHEN DREAMING.

" Are they not all ministering spirits ?"

[The late Leland Stanford, jr., whose example of youthful piety should be a lesson to children of the entire world, always repeated before retiring to rest, the beautiful prayer,—" Now I lay me down to sleep," and invoked the Heavenly blessing upon his beloved parents. The author has taken the liberty to embody this impressive incident in the following poem, feeling, as the Bible teaches, that Heaven and the angels are very nigh to those who believe. It is well known that the Hon. Leland Stanford's princely gift to the State of California, was not only bestowed in commemoration of the memory of his son, but also to carry out the expressed wishes and plans of his child; whose love and consideration for children was only exceeded by his devotion to his dear father and mother.]

An angel came to me when dreaming,
    And whispered fond words, sweet and low;
While on my face the tears were streaming—
    But why those tears I could not know.
Yet, I had lost an earthly treasure
    As pure as flower of earth could be;
And I had loved him beyond measure,
    For he was heaven and life to me.

Now by my side, the angel kneeling—
    I saw the bright form in my sleep—
Prayed reverently, with deepest feeling,
    "I pray thee Lord my soul to keep—
And bless my father and my mother—
    If I should die before I wake—

I love them as I love no other—
　I pray the Lord my soul to take."

Then bending low with fond devotion,
　The holy angel sweetly smiled,
And with a mother's strong emotion
　I knew it was our precious child.
While 'round me golden light was falling,
　Our darling whispered soft and low,
" My angel friends from heaven are calling,
　Kiss me good-night before I go."

Then with angelic touch caressing,
　My lips were pressed with kisses sweet;
And thus in beauty and in blessing
　My heavenly dream was all complete.
And though sometimes my feet may weary
　While walking through the coming years,
The path of life shall ne'er be dreary—
　Since love has been baptised in tears.

Heaven is our trust! there is no other,
　And thus we hear our angel say—
" Look up to Jesus—father, mother;
　His hand shall wipe your tears away."
Our bud of promise still unfolding,
　'Mid fragrance of the life divine;
Beyond the blue, our eyes beholding
　Shall see him rise to manhood's prime.

JANUARY 1st, 1887.

POEM OF WELCOME.

[To Gen. Lucius Fairchild, of Wisconsin, Commander-in-Chief of the G. A. R., read by Comrade W. S. Odell, Washington, D. C., Sept. 23, 1886.]

Hail, our chieftain ! We greet thee with glory to-night,
While around us the stars of Columbia shine bright,
And the stripes of our banner in beauty unfurled
Speak the joy of our nation and pride of the world.
Every star flecked with gold in its heaven-born place,
Every stripe proudly streaming with rapturous grace.
In this soul of the nation, we bid thee good cheer,
For as brothers united we welcome you here.

Yes, welcome, thrice welcome ; we well understand
That we greet thee as one who was born to command,
With the guerdon of Justice and Liberty's dower,
While the blessing of brave hearts gives strength to your power.
Thus the rainbow of love forms an arch overhead
That shall brighten the path where your armies are led—
Men who marched at the sound of the clarion's call ;
Men who laid on the altars of freedom their all.

Hail, our chieftain ! To glory we're marching along ;
Let the sky, air and ocean re-echo our song ;
While our grand institutions, so brilliant in fame,
Speak the triumph our souls would so proudly proclaim.

To our comrades and brothers all over the land
We extend renewed vows, and a firm proffered hand;
That each heart may unite in the interest of all,
Standing true to their trust, when our country shall call !

Hail, our chieftain ! We greet thee and offer to you
The laurel wreath, twined for the noble and true ;
And we pledge you good faith, through the on-coming
    years,
Though our hopes may be dimmed by the memory of tears.
Ah ! brothers, to-night, 'round this banquet outspread,
We are bound by the living and bound by the dead.
By the North and the South, all united and free—
By the deeds of the past, and our works yet to be.

THOU HAST WON MY HEART TO LOVE THEE.

[Music published by John Church & Co.]

Thou hast won my heart to love thee
    The old time dream is past ;
Thy tender, earnest pleading
    Has won my heart at last ;
The brilliant stars of heaven
    That are mirrored in the sea
Cannot be more true and lasting
    Than the love I give to thee.

Thou has won my heart to love thee;
    I bow before love's shrine
And whisper with a trusting heart,
    My darling, I am thine;
And though thou shouldst forget thy vows
    And prove untrue to me,
The heart thou hast so bravely won,
    Will still be true to thee.

Thou hast won my heart to love thee
    And bound me by love's chain,
And through life a willing captive
    I ever shall remain;
And when upon that blissful shore
    My spirit shall be free,
A nobler and a purer love
    I then shall give to thee.

FLOWERS AROUND THE PICTURE.

[Suggested on learning that President Arthur, every morning, wreathes in fresh flowers the portrait of his beloved wife, the late Nellie Herndon Arthur.]

My darling, while around your calm, sweet face,
    I wreathe these precious flowers,
Fond memory bears me with a tender grace
    To life's fair morning hours,

When, like a radiant vision of the skies—
    An angel form divine—
I saw the rapture in your smiling eyes,
    And knew that you were mine.

Hope's rainbow-arch across life's ambient sky
    With heaven was all aglow—
Earth seemed a dream, even heaven itself was nigh,
    For heaven was here below.
Each star that flashed across the azure blue
    From out the dome above
Seemed to our hearts, so trusting and so true,
    A golden gleam of love.

My darling, may this precious wreath of flowers
Remain an emblem of that holier life of ours.
When far above earth's tumult and its strife
Our souls shall meet in God's immortal life,
Where sweet-voiced roses never know decay,
And angel hands shall wipe our tears away.

    WASHINGTON, D, C., *June* 15, 1882.

A SPRAY OF JASMINE.

Within the shadow of my quiet room
      I sit and dream;
While near my casement trembling snowflakes fall
And spread a chilling mantle over all
    The fields, that once were robed in shimmering green.

I dream, and in a far off southern clime
      With fragrance fraught,
I am surrounded by arcadian bowers
Golden with beauty of the jasmine flowers,
    By fairy fingers into garlands wrought.

And through the branches of the waving pines
      And arches dim,
There floats a melody, so sweet and low,
'Tis like unto a river's rythmic flow
    Or grand primeval forest's evening hymn.

And clinging mosses drape the graceful trees
      Just as the veil
Conceals the blushes of the loving bride;
When kneeling proudly by her lover's side
    She vows to love him until life shall fail.

Sweet south-wind whisper low and tell me why
      I thus am blest;
With tranquil joy I view the crimson sky

Whose opal tints upon the ocean lie—
  Like the full glory of a soul at rest.

But ah, though orange groves inspire my dream,
    And perfumed showers
Of sea-kissed roses nestle at my feet—
Without this gift my dream were incomplete,
  Your welcome gift, my friend, of jasmine flowers.

Dear friend, this spray of jasmine speaks to me
    Of summer lands,
And fancy weaves a garland bright and fair
That in the coming years my soul shall wear;
  My dream dissolves, I wake by angel hands.

WE SING OF THE MERRY HARVEST TIME.

SONG.

We sing of the merry harvest time
  When skies are all aglow,
And blossoms of the summer days
  Are drifting scented snow.
And listening to the robin's song,
  Oh, how we love to stray
With bleating flocks and lowing herds
  Down by the new-mown hay.

CHORUS.

We sing of the merry harvest time,
With hearts athrill to music's chime,
Though clouds are dark and tides are low,
We'll dance along and onward go,
Singing of the harvest time.

We sing of the merry harvest time,
  Strange fancies memory weaves,
Of harvesters with dancing feet
  Who gathered golden sheaves.
We love to dream of the reaper's song—
  How bright those memories seem—
When love was young and hope was fair,
  And life was but a dream.

LITTLE EFFIE.

Little Effie, with golden hair,
  Eyes eclipsing the violet's blue;
Lips, like rubies, that always wear
  A smile of brighter and richer hue.

Little Effie, with childish glee,
  Chasing the fleeting hours away;
Radiant, beautiful, fancy free,
  Dancing merrily all the day.

Gathering sunshine, where it lies
   Deep in the lily's cup of gold,
Angels whisper from out the skies:
   "Purer than lily—a thousand fold."

Little Effie, at close of day,
   Bows at the bedside her golden head—
Hear the innocent prattler pray:
   "Bless me before I go to bed."

Oh, that the weary, o'erworn with care,
   Walking life's journey with tired feet,
Would learn from Effie to turn in prayer
   To Heaven for a benediction sweet.

SOME ONE.

Hark! the bell tolling, and crape on the door;
Dear ones are weeping as never before;
Fond hearts are sighing; their joy is all fled,
For the pride of the household lies silent and dead.

Some one was borne by the angels away—
Weary of toiling, no longer could stay;
Some one is robed in a vesture of white,
Who faithfully conquered by doing the right.

Some one has gone from trial and sin
To the land where temptation can enter not in;
Some one has gone to the isle of the blest—
Some one has gone where the weary find rest.

Some one has gone to the beautiful shore,
With angels above, to rejoice evermore.
Saved from all sorrow I know I shall be,
For some one in heaven is waiting for me.

HOW WE JOURNEY.

How oft through life we idly wander
    O'er the green fields with daisies bright,
Where, from the trees, fresh apple blossoms
    Scatter their crowns of pink and white;
Where blushing roses breathe fond kisses
    From lips all moist with scented dew;
'Twould seem that thus, so bliss enchanted,
    We fain would walk life's journey through.

Regardless of the souls who journey—
    Their lives o'ercast with shades of night—
While hopeless tasks and tears of sorrow
    Obscure life's roses from their sight;
With bleeding feet and hands o'erburdened
    With constant toil and withering cares,
While others reap the golden fruitage
    They may but gather up the tares.

A PICTURE OF LIFE.

An exquisite picture I now recall,
That was long ago painted on memory's wall,
Of a fair little babe on its mother's breast,
Who had tenderly closed its blue eyes to rest;
And the chubby hands, with their dimples deep,
Were folded like lilies in infant sleep,
And the artist had touched, with a masterful grace,
Every line on the beautiful sleeper's face.

But the picture has changed, and behold now I see
A golden-haired boy at his mother's knee;
The bright face is all radiant with childish glee,
And the possible hopes that are yet to be.
While the lips seem to whisper, as children can,
"O mamma, I love you! I'm your little man!"
And the mother looks down with a tearful surprise,
For she sees the soul life in her darling boy's eyes.

Now the child turns away and a proud youth appears,
And his eyes speak the promise of oncoming years;
What cares he for the world or the swift-fleeting hours
When his life is all garlanded over with flowers?
His soul is enraptured with life's music sweet,
While he echoes the song with his glorified feet?
And his lips wear a smile, while his heart seems to say,
"I'm a man that the world shall acknowledge some day."

But the youth disappears, and a brave, manly form,
Who has gathered life's harvest in sunshine and storm,
Speaks out from the canvas, and now seems to feel
That the world is a foeman deserving his steel;
And his future is great with the works of the past,
For he knows that men's good deeds are garnered at last;
And he knows life is earnest, if men are but true,
And each heart finds the work which the strong hands
    must do.

Ah! the picture has changed—and now, weary with tears,
I see a form bowed by the gathering years.
The cheek has grown pallid, the footstep is slow,
And the hair is as silver as winter's bleak snow.
But the soul has grown rich in its ocean of grace,
And the eyes look above to the heavenly place
Where his heart's treasures are, and where he, after all,
Shall lovingly answer the good angel's call.

Now the end has drawn nigh, and a bright angel band
Have arrived from the courts of the heavenly land;
But the artist is weeping with soul-throbbing pain,
For he knows that his labor would all be in vain.
For no pencil of artist, nor poet's charmed song,
Could picture the bliss of the seraphim throng;
But we know that we live, and must work for the best,
And can trust to the love of our Father the rest.

TWO NATURES.

There are spirits who walk through life's mystical way,
Ever toiling on wearily day after day,
Looking downward so close to the earth which they tread
That they see not the stars in the sky overhead.
Ah, the hours are so slow and the days are so long—
For they know not the joy of life's wonderful song.
Thus the road is made rough to their slow, plodding feet,
And life's rapturous smiles but a dream incomplete.

There are spirits with wings and they noiselessly fly,
Bearing all of life's burdens aloft to the sky;
And though trials and sorrows around them may throng,
They wake up the world with their heaven-born song.
Like the lark they may rise till they soar out of sight,
Reflecting each star-gem that gladdens the night;
But like dewdrops that fall on the roses at even,
They bring back to the world the sweet perfume of heaven.

Blessed spirits, surrounding with beauty and grace
The mansion of wealth and the humblest place;
All our tears are forgotten and hushed is our fear,
For we know in their presence God's angels are near.
They have learned the true faith, that, without asking why,
It is glory to live, and 'tis glory to die.
Unto them has the record of ages been given,
That the music of earth is the prelude of Heaven.

BLUE MORNING-GLORY.

My blue morning-glory
   All radiant with sweetness—
Your voice like the thrush's song
   Tender and true,
And heart overflowing
   With gentle completeness,
You scatter rich blessings
   In all that you do.

When you swing your blue bells
   From the vine-trellissed bower;
Or come to my window
   To smile in my face,—
You are ever the same pretty
   Summer-kissed flower,
Whose friends all admire you
   For beauty and grace.

But should the south-wind
   Breathe, a message of sadness;
Or clouds in the heavens
   Bring tears to your eyes;
Look within your pure soul
   For the glory and gladness,
That shall brighten your life
   With a joyful surprise.

GENIUS.

Imperial genius, great and grand thou art,
Standing from other lives so wide apart;
The modest veil that drapes your glowing face
Cannot conceal the mastery of your grace.
Oh, genius, where the mellow sunlight streams
And weaves of golden threads a jeweled crown,
And where the holiest star of evening gleams,
There, at thy shrine, I bow in silence down.

And when the lark repeats the song of spring,
And dips in heaven's own blue his fearless wing,
'Till rising thus, above the earth-born throng
He wakes the world with his immortal song;
Around thy brow a halo light is there,
Which makes thy face than angel's face more fair,
Then in thy soul I hear the thought waves throb
And know thou art a prototype of God;

And when I hear the rippling song of June—
A wildwood harp with every string in tune;
When every budding flower is all athrill
With melody which none but June can trill,
And drowsy bees in minor monotone
Kiss the queen lily on her virgin throne;
Oh, then proud genius, kneeling at thy feet,
I find the balm that makes earth life complete.

And when at hush of golden summer day
I see the crimson slowly drift away,
And purple clouds and clouds of amber hue
Sail like good ships across the ethereal blue,
And from the censers of the sleeping flowers
Sweet perfumes rise to charm the evening hours;
Oh! then, loved genius, kneeling at thy shrine
I know the power that blends with life divine.

TWO ALTARS.

I built an altar fair and bright,
 And placed it on the sand;
Its pillars, decked with costly gems,
 Were fashioned by my hand.
Of all things great, on earth or sea,
I said its workmanship should be
 The finest in the land.

When from its censer of pure gold
 I saw the incense rise—
Poor foolish heart, I vainly asked,
 Where is the sacrifice?
A voice came throbbing through my brain:
 "Your altar is but clay."
A wave dashed high upon the shore
 And washed it all away.

Ah, vain is sorrow now, I said,
   And useless is regret;
The clouds that broke my altar down
   Are big with mercy yet.
I turned to Heaven, and asked for help
   To build again once more,
And found the place to build would be
   A rock upon the shore.

Faith, Hope and Love, then helped me rear
   A structure firm and high,
Whose base is built upon a rock,
   Its summit in the sky.
The flowers that round my altar twine
   Shall bloom through all the years,
For when the sunshine dries their leaves
   I water them with tears.

When trials come and storms assail,
   And sorrow leaves its trace,
The rock, whereon my altar stands,
   Shall be my hiding place.

A SHOWER OF ROSES.

In through the casement of my morning room
A breeze steals softly, laden with perfume,
For heaven had rained from out the realms of light
A shower of roses on the world last night.

Bright fairy blossoms, speaking hope and love
To soothe the weary; pointing them above
To the unfading hills, where they may rest
From labor evermore among the blest.

Immortal roses, tell me can it be
You hold within your hearts a shrine for me?
Whisper your answer softly, speak it low,
Sweetest and best of all the flowers that grow.

Oh, precious treasures of the summer time
Your fond reply my soul receives sublime.
While drinking from your lips love's nectar sweet,
You cast your crowns of beauty at my feet.

A shower of roses! coming from the skies,
With fragrant voice you make poor mortals wise;
For speaketh not the rose, with dying breath,
A hope that liveth even after death?

AN AUTUMN DAY.

A stillness rests upon the dreaming hills—
  A glory on the flowers;
It seems to me, this autumn day was born
  Of holier days than ours.

An inspiration from the realms above
  Is borne among the trees,

And fragrant dewdrops from the ambient sky
    Perfume the evening breeze.

The south-wind echoes low in whispered song,
    A chime of vesper bells,
And listening to the music's rippling flow
    My heart with rapture swells.

A holy calm that lights the poet's thought
    Is resting everywhere;
Each trembling blade of emerald grass is fraught
    With fragrant, voiceless prayer.

The autumn leaves, about to say farewell,
    Are robed in gold and rose—
Their transient lives have known earth's fairest charms,
    And none of earthly woes.

The heavens with royal grace are bending low
    In ecstasy divine—
To touch with smiling lips the proffered cup
    Of nature's sparkling wine.

In vain my pen the tranquil scene would trace
    Where angel feet have trod;
I only know, this is a time and place
    To kneel and worship God!

And though the winter days are drawing nigh
    With storms of hail and rain,
The benediction I receive to-day
    Shall keep my heart from pain.

REST, MOTHER, REST.

[In Memory of the Mother of Mr. Samuel G. Kinsiey. Adapted to music by Mrs. Clara Moore, New Philadelphia, O.]

Rest, mother, rest, your care and toil are ended,
    Your trials over and your work well done;
At Heaven's gate, by angel guards attended,
    Your crown was given you—the victory won.
Rest, mother, rest, and peaceful be your slumber,
    Your dear hands folded o'er your gentle breast;
Above your grave shall blessings without number
    Fall from the lips of those your deeds have blest.

Rest, mother, rest, your loving words shall linger
    To soothe and guide us through the coming years,
'Till God shall touch with His eternal finger,
    And turn to joy the fountain of our tears.
Oh, mother, when at holy evening hours
    The stars look down from out the sky of blue,
And dewdrops tremble on the sleeping flowers,
    With reverence then our thoughts shall turn to you.

Rest, mother, rest, your cross is wreathed in roses—
    No brighter joy to child of earth is given,
For while in sleep your precious form reposes,
    Your spirit wakes to nobler life in Heaven.
Oh, gentle south-wind, touch the chords of sweetness
    With tender measure of an artist's hand—

Round mother's grave let music's full completeness
   Echo above to Heaven's sweet summer land.

Rest, mother, rest, we love thee now as ever,
   And though with care our souls may be opprest,
Not even death a mother's love can sever—
   Life's dearest friend, divinest, purest, best.
While by your grave we kneel with strong emotion,
   And breathe our earnest benedictions there,
We know that, when across life's troubled ocean,
   We'll meet again in answer to our prayer.

SWEET VALE OF CONNOTTON.

[The home of the author was for many years in the Connotton valley, in eastern Ohio, and through which flows Connotton creek, whose waters move so slowly as to leave scarcely a ripple upon the surface, excepting in time of heavy rains along the valley, when it overflows its banks and assumes the dignity of a river. The scenery is perfectly charming.]

   Sweet vale of Connotton,
      Ever dear to my soul ;
   Where the soft sunshine plays
      And thy calm waters roll ;
   Others sing of the power
      Of the proud rolling sea ;
   But sweet vale of Connotton
      Thou art heaven to me.

Here the robin trills songs
   To the birds in her nest,
And with tender caresses
   She soothes them to rest,
Then she sings to her mate
   From the juniper tree ;
While sweet vale of Connotton
   Thou art heaven to me.

Ever quietly onward
   Thy calm river flows ;
With a smile on its bosom,
   Of tranquil repose,
And dreaming beside thee
   My spirit is free ;
For sweet vale of Connotton
   Thou art heaven to me.

If from thee, loved valley,
   My footsteps should stray,
And with strangers around me
   Find a home far away ;
Bright and green in loved memory
   Shall thy scenes ever be—
For sweet vale of Connotton
   Thou art heaven to me.

CROCUS.

This morning beside my window
   I heard a voice strangely complete;
A robin was calling her lover
   In words that were thrillingly sweet,

O'er-charmed by the voice of the singer,
   I reverently bowed my head low,
When, behold! a dark-eyed little crocus
   Was peeping from under the snow.

I caught up the fresh little beauty,
   But deep in its pure heart of gold
I knew its young life held a sorrow
   Which had not as yet been told.

For when I pressed fondly its bosom,
   And looked in its heavenly eyes,
The delicate blossom was weeping,
   I found to my tearful surprise.

I asked of the Crocus, sincerely,
   "What giveth your young heart pain?
The roses that sleep close beside you
   Are striving to waken, in vain.

You, of all the fair flowers of my garden,
   Have heard the sweet songs of the spring,
And thus to be favored, believe me,
   Is not such a vain little thing."

The Crocus half folded its petals—
   Thus shading its eyes of dark blue—
And modestly answered, "My story
   Of sorrow, I'll now give to you.

I know that the Crocus is favored,
   To hear the first robin's love song,
And to hear the light feet of the south-wind
   As softly it dances along;

But through all the long lineage of Crocus
   It ever has been our sad lot,
That when roses and lilies were blooming
   The Crocus was always forgot."

Ah, thus it has been and is ever,
   We constantly languish and sigh
For some unattainable blessing,
   Refusing the blessing that's nigh;

And thus a most excellent lesson,
   I never before could know,
I have learned from a plain little Crocus
   Just peeping from under the snow.

IF WE COULD KNOW.

If we could know how many years of life,
Where thorns are growing 'mid the fitful strife,
Our tired feet must walk the weary road

That leads the pilgrim to the unknown abode
Beyond the frontier—oh, if we could know.

If we could lift the veil and bring to view
The hidden page, and read its mysteries through—
Though we were wiser for the knowledge gained,
Would we be happier for the wish attained?
If we could know—ah! yes, if we could know.

If we could know why, in the mystic past
Joy was a dream, too bright and fair to last,
And hope a phantom, mocking all the while
She beckoned us, with weird enchanting smile;
Then left us sorrowing in the vale below.

If we could know where want and woe abide,
And pain is constant at the mourner's side,
Would we make haste to dry the sufferer's tears
And smooth the pathway of the coming years,
Whispering sweet consolation soft and low?

This we can know—we have a work to do,
Though mercy hides the future from our view.
Behold the stars around the crescent rise
To brighten earth with splendor from the skies,
Veiling their faces when the storm winds blow.

The past to us a faithful lesson proves
That while the green earth in her circle moves,
Joy, hope and pain shall journey hand in hand
With faith, the harbor of the heavenly land.
There we shall know—in glory we shall know.

JONQUIL.

Just as the voice of the robin, clear
Warbles the welcome song "spring is here;"
Bright little jonquil in sweet surprise
You peep through the snow with your dreaming eyes.
In your heart of hearts, do the pulse waves swell
As the music floats from your golden bell?
Is there never a heart throb, never a sigh
As you glance from the earth to the far off sky?

Deep down in your bosom to me would seem
A magical throne for a fairy queen;
Where with the soft touch of her delicate hand
She could bless all the flowers in her fairy land.
How pure is the life you so briefly live—
For you ask not a joy for the joy you give—
While you scatter your jewels so rich and rare
Through your kingdom of love, which is everywhere.

Oh! dear little jonquil you speak to me
Of the possible hopes that are yet to be;
For out in the storm where the clouds drop low
You smile through the flakes of enchanted snow.
What cared you for the rain or the winter's cold
As you calmly unfolded your frill of gold;
Then brushing the clouds from your shining hair
You bowed to the world from your golden chair.

Sweet flower so humble and yet so grand,
'Tis well to know you and understand
That modest worth though it hide away
From the glory and pomp of life's summer day;
Is the first to come, when the wintry pall
Of sorrow and storm-clouds around us fall;
And brighten our lives with the soft sunshine
And the tender memories of sweet spring time.

PRETTY LITTLE MAIDEN.

Song.

Maiden, I would speak to thee.
    Pretty little maiden,
On the threshold of thy life,
    Arms with roses laden;
All day long gathering fairest flowers,
    Dreaming not of pain nor care
    In this world of ours.

Maiden, I would tell thee now
    Of approaching danger—
Do not listen to a vow
    Spoken by a stranger.
Blue-eyed maid, fairer than the roses,
    On thy tender, blushing cheek
    Innocence reposes.

Men will worship at thy shrine—
    Maiden dear, believe me—
Calling thee by names divine,
    Only to deceive thee.
Turn away, all their praises scorning
    From the gay deceiver's smile—
    Listen to my warning.

Maiden, I would say "good-bye;"
    May no ill betide thee.
Should the tempter's power be nigh
    Holy angels guide thee,
Safe from harm, pure as morning flowers,
    Dreaming not of pain nor care
    In this world of ours.

OUR SILVER WEDDING SONG.

[Kindly inscribed to Hon. J. L. McCreery and Mrs. McCreery, Washington, D. C., on the occasion of their Silver Wedding.]

Just five-and-twenty years ago
    Our lives were joined together,
To walk through life's mysterious paths
    In calm and stormy weather;
O'er mountain heights and forest glade,
With roses blooming in the shade.

Your eyes so gentle, yet so bright,
   So blissful in their seeming,
Were full of heaven's diviner light,
   Like meadow violets dreaming;
Your lips, like cherries ripe and red,
   So pure in their caressing,
Inspired with every word you said
   New beauty with a blessing.

Your cheeks were like the nectarine
   When summer sunset flushes
The landscape with a crimson sheen—
   It drops its head and blushes.
Your smile was like the golden ray
   That flashes from love's quiver,
And brightened every passing day
   With hopes that live forever.

Your voice, my love, was music sweet,
   My trusting soul entrancing,
As when the brooklet's joyful feet
   Goes o'er the meadow dancing;
But autumn time has only touched
   Your brow with dainty fingers,
For with a pure and hallowed light
   The summer sunset lingers.

My darling, though the faded years
   Were blent with joy and sorrow,
The days that brought us passing tears
   Brought sunshine for the morrow.

And when one darling from the nest
    Fled up to heaven's fair bowers,
Two blushing buds were fondly press'd
    Upon these hearts of ours.

And while our silver wedding bells
    Without are gaily ringing,
The dear old songs that memory tells
    Our loving hearts are singing.
With you, my love, my future hope
    Of happiness reposes;
For you have made life's darkest path
    A very path of roses.

MORNING, NOON, AND NIGHT.

In the morning I gathered fresh flowers
    On the shore of a crimson sea,
When beside me there came a fairy form
    And whispered sweet words to me;
And the music of hope filled the morning air,
While joy with its blessings was everywhere.

But with pain I am now toiling on,
    My tasks growing harder each day,
And I toss my sweet flowers in the dreamy sea
    And with tears see them drifting away.

Ah, why have my hopes fled away so soon,
While yet it is only the hour of noon.

It is night, and the golden stars
   Slowly rise on the amber shore;
And I know I am nearer to Heaven now
   Than I ever was before.
And though summer fades and the winters go
The world is the whiter for winter's snow.

I AM TRUSTING IN GOD.

I am trusting in God,
   And I see the land of glory;
I hear the angels singing from afar;
The words that they sing are the well-remembered story
Of how the heavenly gates were left ajar.
I know my Redeemer is waiting to receive me,
And the day of my rejoicing is begun,
For I hear a sweet voice saying "trusting soul, believe me,
And the work of your salvation is begun."

I am trusting in God,
   And I see the silent river;
I know the ship of Death is sailing near;
But the love of my Saviour shall bear me on forever,
And my happy soul has nothing ill to fear;

Above me I hear precious voices sweetly singing,
Loving spirits are around me everywhere;
Sweet and sweeter the music that in my soul is ringing,
And they tell me I shall meet them over there.

      I am trusting in God,
        For I know that pain and sorrow
And the weary, weary toiling of to-day—
Shall be lost in the brightness of Heaven's grand to-morrow,
When the Master's hand shall wipe our tears away.
All around is the splendor of angels in the chorus;
On the shore, see the shining armies stand,
Of the friends who have conquered and only gone before us
To their rest in the happy Beulah land.

      I am trusting in God;
        Friends farewell, but not forever.
Dearest mother, though our parting gives you pain,
Far beyond the blue sky, where no earthly hand can sever,
We shall meet, and to never part again.
Precious mother, your love like a holy benediction,
Hath so oft given my fainting spirit rest,
And I know that the Lord will sustain you in affliction,
Till you enter in the mansions of the blest.

HIS FOOTSTEP AT THE DOOR.

[Music by Kimball; published by S. Brainard's Sons.]

I am waiting, I am waiting,
    Fondly waiting for my sweet,
Where the evening shadows gather
    For the coming of his feet;
Where daisies white are blooming,
    Like drifts of scented snow,
Where my darling knelt beside me
    In the years of long ago.

In my soul his kisses linger,
    With his voice so sweet and low,
And the fond "good-bye" he whispered
    When he told me he must go.
Will the holy angels guard him
    As they never did before!
While alone I wait the coming
    Of his footstep at the door.

May my prayers to Heaven ascending,
    Hopeful, trusting, pure and true,
Bring to him a benediction
    Gentle as the falling dew;
And the white sail proudly gleaming
    Out upon Love's shimmering sea,
In kind answer to my pleading,
    Bring my darling back to me.

DAFFODIL.

Fragrant little blossom
   Blooming all alone;
Greeting me with gladness,
   Darling little one:
Near thy velvet pillow
   Angel feet have trod,
And thy form was fashioned
   By the hand of God.

Envious little blossom,
   Thus I hear you say—
"Why was I created
   In this plain array?
For I hear the robins
   Laughing as they trill,
'Though an early blossom
   'Tis but a daffodil."

Darling little blossom,
   Beauty, love and grace
Are not always blended
   In a handsome face;
Each one has a station
   He may nobly fill;
Though it may be lowly
   As the daffodil.

MY LITTLE SON AND I.

The sun on the eastern hill-tops
   Is pouring a golden flood,
While evening with smiles advances,
   A queen in her purple robe.
We rest in the flaming splendor
   Dreamily watching the sky,
And our souls are 'rapt in the glory,
   My little son and I.

Higher the crimson rises
   Brighter the flames of gold;
In vain would my soul describe them,
   Such grandeur can ne'er be told.
For only the hand of an angel
   Could paint on the sapphire sky
Those tints that entrance with their beauty
   My little son and I.

But the robe of the evening is fading,
   And hushed is the day-bird's song,
While whippoorwill in the gloaming
   His sorrowful notes prolong.
Yet around us is floating a splendor,
   For we know that e'en heaven is nigh,
And we fold to our hearts each other,
   My little son and I.

WE SILENTLY SLUMBER AT LAST.

This life is a fanciful stage of commotion,
    A dream that is faded and past;
A voyage soon made o'er a storm troubled ocean
    Then we silently slumber at last;
We slumber at last, we slumber at last,
    We silently slumber at last.

From day unto day souls grown weary with pleading
    Have mourned for the hours that are past;
But the poor wounded heart, over weak from its bleeding,
    Shall silently slumber at last,
Shall slumber at last, shall slumber at last;
    Shall silently slumber at last.

Then how can we scornfully jostle each other,
    Or withhold love's endearing repast,
When the people we meet, be they stranger or brother,
    Shall silently slumber at last;
Shall slumber at last, shall slumber at last;
    Shall silently slumber at last.

Oh, then let us give from love's ocean of sweetness,
    Forgetting all wrongs of the past,
Such gems as will bring to us heaven's completeness
    When we silently slumber at last;
When we slumber at last, when we slumber at last,
    When we silently slumber at last.

PRETTY ROBIN-REDBREAST.

[Published in sheet-music form by Annie Pixley, with a picture of Miss Pixley on title page.]

Pretty robin-redbreast
   Near my cottage door;
Asking for a crumb of bread—
   This, and nothing more.
In your sweet contentment,
   Singing me a song,
Where have you been wandering
   All the winter long?

In the maple branches;
   Where the daisies grow;
Where the dancing streamlet
   Murmurs in its flow;
Have you little birdlets
   In a downy nest,
Waiting to be folded
   To their mother's breast?

Pretty robin-redbreast,
   Darling little friend,
Should a note of sorrow
   With your music blend;
Will you not remember—
   Though you sadly sing—
Joy attuned to sadness
   Is a precious thing.

Pretty robin-redbreast,
    Sing your sweet refrain;
Bringing dreams of summer time
    Back to me again;
June with roses laden,
    Fields of yellow wheat,
Rich with summer sweetness,
    Gathered at my feet.

FROZEN.

I gathered some plants with a tender hand,
They were gorgeous as those of a tropical land.
Their censers all laden with rich perfume.
I placed them in pots; for a friend had said,
"If tenderly nursed they will live, and shed
Rich volumes of fragrance, to cheer the gloom
Of the winter days in your quiet room."

An artisan came with a magic hand
And traced on my window panes fairy land—
Gleaming lakes of silver, and mountains of snow.
He labored hard—the wily old wight—
To build up such grandeur in one short night;
Then he told my *green* plants that he loved them so
And said "kiss me good-bye before I go."

Morning arose and bright billows of gold
O'er hill-top, meadow and streamlet rolled;
Through curtains of amber and crimson they shed
Soft roseate tints; a warm summer glow
That strangely contrasted with winter's snow,
But my plants were frozen, their beauty had fled,
And all, save one little rose tree was dead.

Thus many fond hearts, by false love beguiled,
Are drooping and fading in anguish wild;
And no smile of morn, nor crimson bright,
Can bring to their faded cheeks the light
Of other days,—but still lives for me
In its blushing beauty, my fair rose tree.

REST.

There is rest for the weary one
    Rest for the meek;
There is rest near the setting sun
    Rest for the weak.
There is rest for the troubled heart
    Rest for the soul;
Gilead's precious balm
    Maketh us whole.

There is rest where good angels sing
  All the day long;
Where the friends we so dearly love
  Join in the song.
There is rest where the aching heart
  Knoweth no pain—
Where voices of darling ones
  Greet us again.

Then go to the Blessed One—
  Lean on His breast;
Cast your burden of care on **Him**
  Who promises rest.
Kindly He pities you—
  Weeps when you weep,
And when life's tasks are done
  Giveth sweet sleep.

AUTUMN GLORY.

October waves a proud farewell
  With trailing robes of crimson splendor,
And presses with her jeweled hand
  The trembling hand of chill November,
Then bending closer, whispers low,
  In words of more than summer sweetness,
Behold! the promise of the land
  Now garnered in its full completeness!

White curtains drape the western sky,
    Embroidered with the gold of heaven,
While from the amber-tinted folds
    A balmy breeze is softly driven.
A robin sings a parting song,
    And sets the wooded hills a-ringing,
While from the trellis at the door
    The jasmine bells are gently swinging.

Tall spikes of feathered golden-rod
    Are pointing with their jeweled fingers,
Across the emerald fields of wheat,
    Where the rich kiss of summer lingers.
The sun looks on with raptured gaze,
    And like a fond, devoted lover,
He kisses with impassioned grace
    The blushes from late blooms of clover.

Now comes the blissful Hallowe'en
    When holly-branch, a gift possessing,
Reveals the future yet to be,—
    Endowing life with every blessing.
The blushing maid, with guileless heart,
    Turns pale with transport to discover
Reflected in her looking-glass,
    The features of her own true lover.

Pale violets down beneath the sod
    Have closed their eyes so sweetly tender,
To dream of a returning spring
    Regardless of a bleak November.

Nature, still truthful to the last,
    Confirms the oft-repeated story,
That splendor of the summer time
    Can ne'er compare with autumn glory.

OHIO.

Ohio, I love thee, for deeds thou has done;
Thy conflicts recorded and victories won;
On the pages of history, beaming and bright,
Ohio shines forth like a star in the night.
Like a star flashing out o'er the mountain's blue crest,
Lighting up with its glory the land of the west;
For thy step onward marching and voice to command,
Ohio, I love thee, thou beautiful land.

Commonwealth grandly rising in majesty tall—
In the girdle of beauty the fairest of all.
Tho' thunders of nations around thee may roar—
Their strong tidal waves dash and break on thy shore—
Standing prouder and firmer when danger is nigh,
With a power to endure and an arm to defy;
Ohio shall spread her broad wings to the world,
Her bugles resounding and banners unfurled.

A queen in her dignity, proudly she stands,
Reaching out to her sister states wealth-laden hands.
Crown'd with plentiful harvests and fruit from the vine,
And riches increasing in ores from the mine.
While with Liberty's banner unfurled to the sky—
Resolved for the UNION to do or to die—
Her soldiers and statesmen unflinchingly come,
'Mid booming of cannon and roll of the drum.

To glory still onward, we're marching along,
Ev'ry heart true and noble re-echoes the song,
Ever pledged to each other, through years that have fled,
We have hopes for the living, and tears for the dead.
Bless the heroes who suffered, but died not in vain;
Keep the flag that we love—without tarnish or stain.
Thus uniting with all, shall my song ever be
Ohio, my home-land, my heart clings to thee!

COME WHERE THE FLOWERS LIE SLEEPING.

Come where the flowers lie sleeping
    Down in their crystal beds;
Come where the shy little violets
    Are resting there weary heads.
Come in the early morning,
    Come in the fading gray,
Come where the painted rose-tints
    Reveal the sweet smiles of day.

Come in the golden noontide;
   Pause where the blossoms sleep;
Dreaming of last year's blushes,
   And the tears that e'en flowers must weep.
Hope for the coming springtime
   With its incense of fragrant dew,
When winter shall drop its mantle
   And bring the fresh flowers to view.

Come in the hush of evening—
   Come with a noiseless tread;
Whisper of loving caresses
   Oft-given the flowers we call dead.
For soon shall the birds in the branches
   Awaken with musical trill,
The eyes of each delicate blossom
   Whose pulses of life are still.

Come when the heart in its anguish
   Bleeds for the dearest and best,
Who faded when summer was fading
   And folded her pure hands to rest.
Turn to the beautiful city—
   Oh, there, let your anguish'd soul rise,
Where the fair flower, your loving heart cherished,
   Wakes to life in the heavenly skies.

FOR ME, SWEET BIRDS.

While nature pours its choicest gifts
   Into the lap of June,
And flowers awakened at her voice
   Come laden with perfume;
Oh, sing your songs for me, sweet birds,
   Your tender, trusting, loving words,
Whose music thrills my soul with joy,
   Light-hearted, happy birds.

Your mystic rhymes of ecstasy,
   Fall softly on my ear;
They tell me winter's power is past
   And summer now is here.
Oh, sing your songs for me, sweet birds,
   There's magic in your loving words,
And summer would not summer be
   Without your songs, sweet birds.

You bear me back to childhood's hours,
   Those long departed years,
And though I love to hear your songs,
   My eyes grow dim with tears.
But tears are hallowed mysteries
   Our lives would fain conceal,
And thus your soul-enchanting words
   Oft dearest hopes reveal.

THERE IS A DIFFERENCE.

There is a difference, though the sun's bright rays
   Shine on the just and unjust alike,
And unto each are given equal days,
   Still we divine not Heaven's mysterious ways.

There is a difference, oft vainly the good may toil
   To give beloved ones comfort, and sweet rest;
Remorseless penury may like a serpent coil
   And blighting weeds o'ergrow the fertile soil.

There is a difference, virtue so often blamed
   Shrinks from the heartless gaze of cruel scorn,
While laurels and glad songs have oft proclaimed
   Honors all undeserved to those who attained.

The unjust man, with inteilectual power
   May classify the stars and call their names,
Unfolding each bright page of hidden lore
   While rustics wonder all the more and more.

But he may languish on a couch of pain,
   His friends dark-eyed Remorse and fierce Despair,
His sins upon him like a withering flame—
   Heaven's birthright sold, for greed of earthly gain.

Repine not faithful soul, by care oppressed,
   Hard is the battle—but soon victory won
Shall blazon thy banners. Heaven's imperial crest
   Shall point the way to God's eternal rest.

EMANCIPATION DAY.

[Read by Milton Holland at the Emancipation Banquet, Washington, D. C., April 13th, 1883.]

Sound aloud the trump of freedom,
Let the answering echo ring,
While with liberty commanding,
We our heartfelt tribute bring;
As we gather round Columbia,
Let us scatter on the way
Flowers of love and flowers of trusting,
For Emancipation Day.
Let us pray for benedictions
While we bow in reverence low
At the shrine of noble heroes,
Bravely charging on the foe.
Gladly we hear our welcome,
To this feast of Liberty.

WELCOME.

Lo, the car of progress moving,
Over all Columbia's land;
Gifted men are proudly coming
And we take them by the hand—
Men of different race and color,
Yet our peers in soul and brain,
And their names shall soon be sculptured
On the towering dome of fame.

Float aloft the stars of glory,
For we love to tell the story
That is written on the pages
Of Columbia's record true;
How amid the cannon's rattle,
And the shot and shell of battle,
Chains of living death were broken
By our gallant boys in blue!

Ah! our soldiers never faltered;
Never heeded they the gloom;
Quailed not when the shock of battle
Seemed the eternal knell of doom;
But with comrades pale and bleeding
Only heard Columbia pleading —
" Wipe away from my escutcheon
Every trace of human woe.
Let my rightful sons and daughters
Of whatever race they be,
Hear the clarion voice of heroes,
Making way for liberty.

Let no cloud of dark oppression
Linger in Columbia's sky;
Let the joyful shout of freedom
Rise aloft to God on high!"

Days were dark and fierce the struggle—
Can it be the day is lost?

Came from many an anguished mother,
As she reckoned up the cost
Of the blood and of the treasure,
Given freely without measure,
As the price of liberty.

But amid the desolation,
Spreading o'er our glorious land
Came the news—Emancipation
Has been reached—the proclamation,
Far above the cannon's roar
Sounded loud, o'er hill and valley
Bells were ringing, hearts were singing,
As they never sung before.

For the shackels had been broken,
And four million souls were free,
That 'till then had never tasted
Of the joys of liberty!
And to-day we gladly greet them,
As we gather 'round to meet them,
And to take them by the hand—
Men whose throbbing souls ignited
At the watch-fires freedom lighted.
Freedom's altar fires, still burning
Flash and sparkle at each turning,
As the car of progress moving,
Rolls them on to nobler fame.

A WINTER DAY.

Beside my cottage, in their towering height,
Rise purple hills, crowned with a sunset light;
Kissed by a breath of such peculiar sweetness
That heaven bows down, in all its grand completeness.
The western sky is flecked with drops of gold—
Richer by far than poet's song has told—
In vain a painter's art would dare portray
The glowing splendor of the closing day.

But ah! the trees in seeming desolation,
Lift up their hands in feeble supplication;
Yet with the prayer this hopeful thought is blended—
"To us, the day of beauty is not ended;
Though from our arms the whispering leaves are fled
Within our hearts the life-power is not dead;
Soon from our branches shall the wild birds sing
Amid the foliage of the coming spring."

Ever thus, our souls so subject to temptation,
We gladly know are not our own creation.
Though ruthless hands our dearest joys may sever—
Trusting in God we shall not fail, no never.
And should we work through years of vain endeavor
The victor's wreath shall crown the bright forever,
And hopes that now lie faded at our feet
Shall bloom again, in endless fragrance sweet.

MY LOVE OF LONG AGO.

[Music by Bischoff, published by John Church & Co.]

Down by the silvery sea to-night
　　The sky is all aglow,
And crowned by evening's golden light
　　The sparkling breakers flow;
And I am waiting for my love—
　　As dear as life can be—
Oh, winds that float from heaven above,
　　Pray bring him back to me.

'Twas down beside the silvery sea
　　On that sweet summer day,
My lover pledged his vows to me,
　　And then he sailed away.
Ah, I have waited through the years,
　　And watched the sails go by,
And cherished hopes with all my tears,
　　But yet, no ship is nigh.

Oh, sweet south-wind beside the sea,
　　I ask this boon of you,
Go tell my lover this for me—
　　That still my heart is true,
And may the holy angels guide
　　His steps where'er they go,
And Heaven grant no ill betide
　　My love of long ago.

MY LOVE IS TRUE TO ME.

ANSWER TO MY LOVE OF LONG AGO.

Song.

My darling I have heard your song
   And know your prayers for me,
And know that you have waited long
   And watched beside the sea.
And while my barque is sailing home
   Bright, with its freight of gold,
Your voice of love that bids me come
   Is more a thousand fold.

Your love has been my guiding star
   Though clouds might intervene ;
It whispers softly from afar,
   As meadow violets dream.
And though I sail the stormy sea,
   My soul is all for you—
What greater joy of earth can be
   When you my love are true?

Soon 'neath the glowing western sky,
   We'll anchor in the bay,
And then with joy my love and I
   Shall name the happy day.
With memory's golden chain secure,
   My darling's life shall know,
My vows of love and faith are pure
   As in the long ago.

A REVERIE.

[Dedicated to Welch Post, G. A. R., Department of Ohio.]

The year draws near its close, and in the sobbing air,
We hear the voice of winter everywhere;
Within our homes the cheerful embers glow,
While softly falls the winter's crown of snow.
The ripened harvests garnered safe away,
Secure us plenty for each coming day,
And thus, with grateful hearts our thanks are given
To Him who gives us home and gives us heaven.

How short the years are—seeming but a day
Since men, as comrades, bravely marched away;
For they had heard the ominous tocsin bell
That tolled a dirge, when proud Fort Sumter fell.
Their partings said—then mothers, sisters, wives
Bade them God speed, with tender, tearful eyes;
While sweethearts blushed and tried in vain to still
The heart-throbs, that each loving word would thrill.

The strongest comrade shed a manly tear,
When low sweet words revealed the parting near;
And men who braved the cannon's thundering roar
Trembled and faltered at the roof-tree door.
But on the field, where, battle-stained and torn
The glorious flag of liberty was borne
By stalwart hands—all danger to defy—
The shout went up, "For liberty we die."

Ah, how the loved ones, waited day by day
For messages from heroes far away;
And how they wept, no poet's pen can tell,
To read the record, how some hero fell.
Year after year the shock of battle rang
Throughout the land, and brought each heart a pang;
And graves were made, amid our hopes and fears,
And loyal blood was mingled with our tears.

We sometimes felt our prayers were all in vain;
The roll was called—"three hundred thousand slain!"
But God knew best, and gave our eyes to see
The golden light; four million souls were free!
And we to-day can boast the honored name
Of gallant men who fell among the slain—
One on the field, and one passed on above
While teaching Heaven's ministry of love.*

And while the years go by, with birds and flowers,
We'll ne'er forget these comrades brave of ours;
When reveille proclaims the morning light,
Or tattoo sounds, 'mid gathering shades of night;
Or when 'round camp fire we together meet,
To make unwritten history more complete—
Memory will bring anew the tearful scene,
How we, on duty, shared the same canteen.

* Welch Post was named in honor of two brave soldiers who were residents of Tuscarawas county, Ohio.

And when God's armies muster into line
With angels, worshipping at the eternal shrine ;
WELCH POST will "forward march" at tap of drum,
And hear the plaudit, faithful souls "well done."
With comrades brave from over all our land
We'll marshal forces at the Great Command,
In solid colum, rank and file shall rest,
In heavenly armor, helmet, shield and crest.

MARGUERITE.

[Music by Bischoff, published by John Church & Co.]

Star-eyed flow'ret, Marguerite,
You have wakened from your dream,
In the meadow by the stream—
Where the laughing little brook
(Brighest page in nature's book)
Heard the lily from its throne—
In a gentle undertone—
Whisper to itself alone ;
" Marguerite, Marguerite."

Star-eyed flow'ret, Marguerite,
Have you loving words to tell,
Of the pleasant woodland dell,
Where the violet in surprise

Opened wide its dreaming eyes;
When the fairies' dancing feet,
And the thrushes' music sweet,
Made your humble life complete,
Marguerite, Marguerite.

ON THE EVERGREEN SHORE.

[In Memory of Miss L. W. F.]

Oh sweet be thy slumber, my darling,
   In Heaven thy loved spirit shall rest
From sorrow and sin and temptation,
   At home with the saints ever blest.
Oh, zephyrs of spring-time float softly,
   And wake not her gentle repose,
Whose life like a bright flower unfolded—
   Like a swift fading flower was its close.

I knew that her dear life was fading,
   As a rose when it blushes at even,
When kissed by the breath of the summer
   That wafts its sweet perfume to heaven;
For when shadows of evening were falling,
   And the stars lighting up the blue sky,
Angel voices around her were calling,
   I heard their soft wings rustle by.

While on through life's tiresome journey,
   I wearily toil day by day,
I'll trust in the blessed Redeemer,
   And think of my child when I pray;
My darling, as fair as the roses
   That bloom with the coming of spring;
Whose dear form in silence reposes
   Where birds of the summer-time sing.

Far away is a beautiful river
   That flows by the evergreen shore,
Where the angels make music forever,
   And where friends meet to part nevermore.
And I know that my child will be waiting
   On the banks of that river for me;
When I hear the blest words of our Saviour,
   "Welcome home, for thy spirit is free."

THE RECOMPENSE OF FAITH.

I had struggled in the darkness—
   In the darkness of the night;
While no ray of golden sunshine
   Shed its gleam of glorious light.
And when fain among the reapers,
   I would gather up the sheaves,
I could only find before me
   A few dead and withered leaves.

While my hands were worn and weary,
    And my feet with thorns all scarred,
And the lessons suffering taught me,
    Were both practical and hard;
Still I knew that God intended
    That my hands should gather flowers;
Else why were they strewn so thickly
    In this changeful world of ours?

Thus with patient faith I waited;
    Trusting on from day to day,
'Till I found my path grow brighter,
    For the clouds were giving way.
Then I knelt before the Master,
    And with trembling and with tears
I revered Him for the mercy,
    That had kept me through the years.

Through the weary years of trial,
    When no earthly friend was nigh
To relieve my heavy burdens,
    Nor to hear my pleading cry.
Now I ask for grace to keep me
    Till my tasks of life are done;
Till life's work shall all be ended,
    And the crown of victory won.

REST, NOBLE HERO, REST.

[Read Memorial Day, 1884, at the grave of Col. Alfred B. Meacham, of Modoc fame.]

Rest, hero, rest, thy care and toil is done,
Thy battle ended and thy victory won;
Thy path through life was often dark and drear,
Yet faith's eternal lamp was bright and clear;
Thy trusting soul in darkest hours would stand
Amid the joy of Heaven's sweet summer-land.
Though thou did'st suffer much and suffer long,
Pain always made thy dauntless spirit strong,
And 'mid the storms of sorrow's wild unrest,
They always loved thee most who knew thee best.

Friend of the friendless ones, whose council fires
Burn low in memory of departed sires;
Who, in the solemn grandeur of the wood
Hear the Great Spirit whisper, Heaven is good;
Whose faith sublime with ours might well compare;
For unto them God dwelleth everywhere.
'Tis true, they sent the bullet in the fray,
To take from thee thy precious life away;
But when they found thee still their faithful friend,
They loved thee well and loved thee to the end.

Rest, hero, rest, we love thee now, as in departed years,
While on thy grave we place these flowers and bless them
    with our tears,

The bugle call can never wake thee from thy dreamless sleep,
But angel forms around thy grave shall loving vigil keep.
The balmy breeze at evening time shall chant a requiem song,
And woodland thrush in gentle tones the sacred notes prolong.
These flowers will drift their fragrant snow across thy silent breast,
While nature's voices whisper low, rest, noble hero, rest.

WHAT IS POETRY.

Go ask the rose, whence came its shapely grace
And the rich blushes of its smiling face,
And why its leaves such holy incense shed
When all of beauty, life and hope are dead.
And why we cherish through departing years
Its memory, with our blessings and our tears.

Go ask the lily in its stately pride,
Or when it dips its fingers in the tide;
Why it was formed to neither toil nor spin,
Yet more than kingly glory here to win.
And when its trusting heart to heaven looks up,
The bee drinks nectar from its brimming cup.

Go ask the violet, humble, pure and true,
Who gave to it its eyes of tender blue,
And such rare sweetness, that the angels tread
With reverent awe beside its lowly bed;
And when 'tis crushed by cruel, careless feet,
It only smiles and breaths a sigh more sweet.

Go ask the birds why they in chorus sing
The same sweet words with each returning spring,
And soaring upward from ambrosial bowers
Look down upon this careworn world of ours;
While white-winged beings, near heaven's portal throng
To listen to the glory of their song.

Go ask the stars, enrobed in golden light,
Who gave to them a voice to rule the night,
And myriad banners flashing o'er the sea,
Reflecting heaven's eternal imagery;
While man looks up with wonder from afar
To view the splendor of each royal star.

Go ask the worn with waiting, weary heart,
That in life's trials bears a bitter part,
Whence comes the rainbow light across the skies
Revealing roseate tints of Paradise.
And the sweet voice, the gentle "peace be still,"
That calms its fears and makes its pulses thrill.

Go ask of these, thus shall the answer be,
" There blooms a flower immortal—Poetry.

God gave it man, to make his pathway bright,
And hide the thorns and thistles from his sight.
With awe we worship, at the rose-wreathed shrine,
And bow before an influence Divine!"

THE OLD HEARTHSTONE.

[Music published by Shaw & Co.]

SONG.

I'm dreaming of the old hearthstone;
   The home so far away,
And pleasant scenes that long have flown
   Come back to me to-day.

Chorus.

The old hearthstone, the old hearthstone—
   While sailing o'er life's restless sea
Shall memories of the old hearthstone
   Bring joy and hope to me.

I see the maples by the mill
   The orchard and the lane;
The cherry trees upon the hill
   Seem all to be the same.

Beside the hearth my mother sits,
   Her face so calm and fair;
Her hands the self-same stocking knits
   As when I last was there.

The rockers of her old arm-chair
    Are making music sweet;
The kitten with its glossy hair
    Is nestling at her feet.

And yet I know that twenty years
    Have with their blessings fled,
And on a marble stone appears
    The name of 'mother'—dead!

Dear mother sleeps, no throb of pain
    Her loving heart can stir—
Our loss was her eternal gain,
    We need not weep for her.

But while these sacred memories rise
    With dreams of home, sweet home,
Tears come unbidden to my eyes,
    While o'er the world I roam.

A SONG OF SADNESS.

They are blooming in their beauty—
    The early flowers of spring,
And above my cottage window,
    I hear the wild birds sing;

But the flowers will fade and leave us
  Though the smiles of sunlight fall,
And the tender dew of heaven
  Sheds it's sweetness over all.

'Twas thus, the joys of spring-time
  That blossomed in a day,
'Neath the chilling winds of autumn
  Were buried, all away;
And the hopes I love to cherish
  Are hidden in my pain,
For I sigh to think life's summer-time
  Can never come again.

Cease, my soul, thy wail of sadness
  There is work for thee to do;
Though the cruel storms of winter
  Hide life's roses from thy view,
It is only the faint-hearted
  Who yield to blank despair,
While the true and noble gather
  Gems of beauty everywhere.

TELL ME ROSES.

SONG.

Oh, tell me, shining lilies,—
   Let me press your hand of snow,—
Does my lover love me truly?
   For surely you must know.
In the early gray of morning
   When your lips were wet with dew—
Did not an unseen angel come
   And whisper it to you?

Oh, tell me blushing roses
   With your voice of fragrance sweet,
Tell me will my absent lover
   Come and worship at my feet?
I have been so broken-hearted
   Since we pledged our fond good-bye,
And if he has ceased to love me—
   Tell me roses, tell me why.

Oh, brilliant stars of heaven
   That gem the brow of night,
Go brighten up his pathway
   While absent from my sight.
Oh, fairy winds float softly
   While you cross the distant sea,
And pray tell my absent lover
   To hasten back to me.

SUMMER WEATHER.

Across the fields of ripening grain
    The smiles of summer light are glancing,
And on the river's silver breast
    The shadows of the trees are dancing,
As on the chanting waters flow,
    The lilies dream and sigh and quiver
And dip their snowy finger-tips
    Into the sweetly singing river.

The humming birds, in rainbow sheen,
    Drink nectar from the fragrant clover,
And from the vale the meadow-lark
    Is calling for her truant lover.
The summer skies and river's song
    And music of the woodland thrushes,
Bring back the hour when first I kissed
    From my love's cheek the tell-tale blushes.

Heaven bless the time our vows were given
    To walk the path of life together,
Through autumn shades and wintry storms
    And dreamy bliss of summer weather.
The stars bore witness to our pledge,
    And bowed their crowns of golden glory,
As though 'twere something new to hear
    From lover's lips the old, old story.

Full twenty years have come and gone,
    And brought us tears as well as pleasure,
What matters it—I still possess
    My purest, dearest, only treasure.
Sing thrushes! let your songs and mine,
    Blended in unison together,
Rehearse the sweetness of to-day—
    The splendor of this summer weather.

SOMETIME.

Sometimes my heart and brain grow very weary
    Longing for quiet rest;
Life seems to be a desert dark and dreary
    With fragant flowers unblest.

Sadly I sigh for fields of scented clover
    Where wild bees love to roam;
In vain I search the beds of violets over
    To find one leaf of bloom.

If I could hear one strain of music thrilling,
    My glad enraptured soul
Would bow at life's behests, supremely willing,
    Till love should make me whole.

E'en o'er my muse a cloud of gloom is drifted—
   Coldly enshrouding all ;
I wonder if the cloud will e'er be rifted
   At memory's loving call.

Ah, heart ! so ever ready at repining,
   God doeth all things best ;
Sometimes He hides the gorgeous silver lining
   To give His children rest. -

Else our poor eyes o'erdazzled by the splendor
   Would soon grow weak and dim ;
He wills it thus, no earthly arm can hinder—
   Then learn to trust in Him.

Sometime, beyond the golden gates of glory
   My soul shall learn to know
Why life was thronged with deserts wierd and hoary
   And always clouded so.

SEA–ANEMONES.

Anemones ! sea-anemones,
   Purple, white and red,
Dreaming loves enchanted dream
   In your golden bed ;

Memory bears me back again
   'To your fragrance sweet,
Where the cool waves of the sea,
   Danced beside my feet.

Anemones! sea-anemones,
   Tell me can it be
We shall ever meet again
   Close beside the sea?
Where the breakers proudly rise,
   Towering mountain high,
While the silver-crested foam
   Drapes the azure sky.

Blessed hours, when love and I
   Wandered hand in hand,
And the ocean seemed to be
   Love's immortal land;
Listening to the trembling sea's
   Sacred monotone,
This my lover said to me—
   "Will you be my own?"

While the answer of my soul
   Blushing lips concealed,
Quick the throbbing of my heart
   Loving words revealed.
Voice of love is still the same,
   Though it silent be;
Thus my raptured heart confessed—
   'Twas no longer free.

Anemones! sea-anemones,
  Purple, white and red,
Dream for other lovers now
  In your golden bed.
While you close your tearful eyes
  Dreaming life away—
Other lovers by the sea,
  Roam love's land to-day.

THE VOICE OF THE ROSES.

Oh! this precious gift of roses—
  They shall droop and fade away,
For each heart of gold discloses
  Trembling signs of sure decay.
But in death they breathe a sweetness
  Through this throbbing life of mine,
And 'mid suffering's full completeness,
  I shall know their power sublime.

Oh! this precious gift of flowers
  Speaks a world of joy to me—
Tells me of the golden hours
  And the days that used to be;
Days when yet my footsteps lingered
  In the Eden of the blest—
When each passing zephyr whispered
  Only love and hope and rest.

Oh ! this precious gift of flowers
  . Fill my soul with sweet surprise,
And in fancy, Heaven's fair bowers
    Bloom, before my wondering eyes;
While with reverent gaze and holy
    As I look toward the sky,
Clouds above me, drifting slowly,
    Seem like angels passing by.

Oh ! this precious gift of flowers
    Speaks of glorious victories won ;
Whispers of the restful hours
    When the battle's toil was done.
Speak, oh flowers, with voice of sweetness,
    Words that oft the weary thrill—
Fraught with God's supreme completeness,
    " Peace, oh troubled heart be still."

THE RIVER'S ANSWER.

White-winged and beautiful, swift flowing river,
Chanting thy sweet songs forever and ever ;
Pause in thy music, and tell me I pray
Whither on white wings so swiftly away.

Ever thou bringest me dreams of my childhood,
When from thy shore near the deep-tangled wildwood,
River and sky softly blended together
In the calm twilight of sweet summer weather.

Sometimes in day dreams I am flying like thee,
On thy bright dancing course to the deep-sounding sea;
Sometimes my tired soul rises up in its flight
And enters the mystical portals of light.

Sometimes, ah, sometimes I seem free from life's clod,
And thus in my transport hold commune with God.
Thus blest, through the realms of blue ether I fly,
Too happy to live, but unwilling to die.

Oh, beautiful river, tell me, I implore,
Hast thou ever yet found a flower-bedecked shore,
Where hope was immortal and joy was supreme,
Where no shade of sadness could darken thy dream?

The river reflecting the blue of the sky,
In a voice of strange melody makes this reply.
"There is but one land where the worn and opprest,
The weak and the weary have ever found rest;
This land to the poor of earth's children is given—
'Tis the city of God—the unchangeable heaven."

I ENVY NOT.

I envy not kings the sceptre bright,
Nor crowns encircled with jeweled light,
Nor kingdoms of countless wealth untold,
With hoarded treasures of molten gold.
     I am free—I am free!
The wealth that is born of the soul for me.

I envy not those imperial heads
Where beauty its mystical influence sheds;
Nor voices that murmur sweet words; as the dove
When its heart has been bound in the meshes of love.
     I am free—I am free!
The beauty that comes from the soul for me.

I envy not the rich nor the great,
Who boast of a high and a proud estate;
Nor the cottager his vine-clad cot,
With the greatness and joy of his humble lot.
     I am free—I am free!
The joys of my own sweet home for me.

If envy at all, I only should,
The noble heart, that is truly good;
Who pities the weakness of human lives
And seeks not itself to aggrandize.
     I am free—I am free!
The wealth that is born of the soul for me.

INAUGURATION ODE.

March 4, 1881.

Ring the bells throughout the Nation,
Let the people's grand ovation
  On the tide of music roll;
While our bugles are resounding,
And all loyal hearts are bounding,
Let the fire-tongue flash the message
  Through the earth from pole to pole.

Greet our chieftain with a blessing,
While the winds of Heaven caressing
  Sing their songs of welcome low;
Grand triumphal arches bending,
And with sweetest incense blending,
Scatter beauty o'er his pathway,
  Like to drifts of perfumed snow.

Hail! the stars and stripes of glory
Wake anew to tell the story
  Of the vict'ries we have won;
How amid the thundering rattle,
And the shot and shell of battle,
Proudly stood our brave defenders
  Till their noble work was done.

Heaven be praised, the time is ended
    When the clarion's giant breath
Sounded loud, to call our comrades
    To the rank and file of death.
Crown the dead and bless the living—
    All who struggled to be free;
Bless the men who marched with Sherman
    From Atlanta to the sea.

Brothers, let us stand united,
    Firm and true in heart and hand;
North and South, in solid column,
    Pledged, a strong fraternal band.
Nations bow their heads to listen
    To the pledge we make to-day,
While we fold the blue around us,
    And forget the fading gray.

Lo! the lamps of peace are burning,
And the olive branch returning,
Welcomes all the States together
    To this festival of love.
Greeting, trusting, we assemble
While the list'ning nations tremble;
For they know Columbia registers
    Our pledge of faith above.

On to glory, pass the watchword
    Through the lines from shore to shore;
Not a soul must dare to falter—
    On to glory evermore!

While our signal lights are flashing,
Ocean breakers, wildly dashing,
Cannot, dare not reach Columbia,
   On her pedestal secure.

Ring the bells throughout the Nation ;
Let the people's grand ovation
   On the tide of music roll ;
Echo hill and dale and valley ;
Freemen rally, rally, rally !
While Columbia shouts the watchword
   Through the earth, from pole to pole.

BEAUTIFUL VIOLETS.

Beautiful violets why do you sleep,
   Wrapped in your mantle of snow?
Do you fear the rude touch of the cruel storm-king,
   Or the cold winds that fitfully blow?

Are you waiting to hear the robin's sweet voice,
   From the old orchard tree on the hill ;
While woodland and valley, mountain and glen
   Re-echo the fanciful trill?

Do you dream of the hours we spent by the lake,
   With our old friends the musical birds ;
When from the meadows with daisies o'er spread,
   Came the lowing of numberless herds?

Night after night, the dream angels bring
   Sounds of your silvery feet;
Your fairy-like lips with warm kisses glow,
   Then hope's full fruition's complete.

Beautiful violets' soon from your sleep,
   Blushing with tender surprise
You'll awake, to behold nature radiant and gay,
   With a glance from your wonderful eyes.

A FRAGMENT.

Watching, watching, thoughtfully watching
   Children enjoying their midsummer play;
Dreaming of childhood's ineffable hours
   That on light wings passed quickly away.

Toiling, toiling, incessantly toiling—
   Wearing the gathering hours away;
But when from our grasp they drift away slowly,
   We gladly would welcome their stay.

Hoping, hoping, earnestly hoping
   For flowers that shall bloom at the foot of the hill;
When we reach the low valley where sunlight is fading.
   And have suffered the good Master's will.

HEAVEN BLESS THE LITTLE BOYS.

When out upon the crowded street
  The mischief-loving boys I meet;
Rolling their hoops and tossing ball,
  Ever engaged with busy feet,
I breathe a prayer—Heaven bless them all.

The pride and glory of the town
  Are the bare-foot boys with cheeks of brown;
Who rush along with clamorous noise,
  And hearts as light as eider-down.
Heaven bless them all; those precious boys.

In each young brow and tender face
  And smiling eyes and voice I trace,
The future of our country joys,
  And grand ennobling of our race.
Heaven guard and keep the little boys.

If we would train with honor great,
  Men to adorn both church and state,
And every power of vice destroy,—
  Our prayers must be, early and late,
Heaven's angels guard each little boy.

FAREWELL TO THE OHIO EDITORS.

[In the winter of 1881 a brilliant reception was given to the Ohio Editors visiting Washington, D. C.]

Farewell, sons of Ohio, proud knights of the pen,
As you go to your sanctums to labor again,
From this home of the Union, where Liberty stands
With her arms wide extended and warm loving hands
Reaching out to receive you, and crown you anew
With the laurels reserved for the noble and true.
Go forth, noble toilers, in grandeur of might,
Your laurels emblazoned with truth and the right.

Great men of our nation surrounded your shrine
And poured on your altars the tribute divine
Of their grand inspiration, like garlands of flowers
Kissed by heaven's pure sunlight in sweet morning hours.
'T is thus you go forth, borne on intellect's tide,
With the fires fresh kindled of honor and pride.
Firm and true to your calling your hosts shall be led
With the banner of freedom above you outspread.

Farewell, sons of Ohio, 'tis yours to defend
The proud rights of the people; and thus, to this end,
You must labor for statesmen and soldiers, and all
Who'll be true to their trust when our nation shall call.
With your hands on the pulse of Columbia, to tell
When her heart's blood is throbbing with victory's swell,—
May you bury the sword 'neath our banner unfurl'd,
For the Press is the beacon that lights up the world.

IN SILENCE NOW.

[Mr. L. W. Kennedy, editor of "The Truth," died at his home in Washington, D. C., Feb. 25, 1881. On the coffin was placed a pen made of English violets, and the chief mourner was his intended bride.]

    Fold the cold hands of the sleeper;
        Walk with silent step and slow;
    Breathe a parting benediction—
        Holy, reverent, sweet and low.
    Press love's purest, fondest kisses
        On the tear-wet, marble brow:
    'Tis a fitting time for worship,
        Bow the knee and worship now.

    Hushed the voice; the bright expression
        Faded from the love-lit eyes—
    But the soul in holier radiance
        Smiles from Heaven's immortal skies.
    Heard you not the benediction,
        Heard you not the harps of gold,
    When the angel song of welcome
        Through the heavenly portals rolled?

    When we heard the white wings rustle
        And the sigh of parting breath,
    Then we wept in sobbing anguish,
        For we said the sleep was death.

What is death?   'Tis like a lily—
    Spotless, fragrant, white and pure.
Need death seem so cold and chilly
    Since it makes our faith secure.

Let him rest, the noble toiler—
    Earnest champion of "The Truth,"
While the pen of fragrant violets
    Writes the words, "immortal youth."
In the land of deathless flowers,
    Emblems of a woman's love,
These fond hearts shall be united
    Evermore in Heaven above.

CENTENNIAL ODE.
JULY, 1876.

Unfurl your banners, let the joy-bells ring;
All hail the light that heralded the dawn,—
The glorious dawning of our greatness;
Ring, ring the bells and let the echo run
To every kindred land beneath the sun;
Let all unite, to celebrate the day
When smiling Heaven in kindly mood bestowed
Our own beloved,—immortal Washington!

Unfurl the stripes, float out the golden stars,
Emblem of more than life,—our liberty,

The priceless boon for which our fathers bled,
And bravely died, on to the conflict led,
By him who, patriot, statesman, soldier all combined
Now lives, within a nation's heart, enshrined.

We speak his name, and every pulse is thrilled
From very love, our eyes with tears are filled;
Born to be honored—seeking not renown,
His noble brow disdained to wear a crown.
He needed none, his own great deeds shall be
A living crown through all eternity!
And nations yet unborn, shall honor claim,
To bow their heads, and proudly speak his name.

Our Washington! well may our pulses thrill,
Well may bright eyes, with loving tears o'erfill
For him, who lit Columbia's torch of fame,
And dying bequeathed her sons his honored name.

*　　*　　*　　*　　*　　*

But hark! commotion sounds throughout the land,
Dismay and terror reign on every hand;
Fort Sumpter falls, 'mid showers of shot and shell—
Blood marks the spot where Sumpter's heroes fell.
Brother meets brother in the unholy strife;
Each madly strives to take the other's life;
Columbia mourns,—her proud escutcheon stained—
Drooping the wreath her fallen heroes gained.

But joy! above the din of war, is heard
The welcome news,—each loyal heart is stirred,

The angel Peace, outspreads her golden wings;
The dove, the olive branch of covenant brings.
Rejoice, for North and South are bound as one;
"With charity for all, and malice toward none!"
Brothers again!—hushed is the knell of doom,
Where tumult raged, love's fairest flowers bloom.

Ring, ring the bells, and let the echo run
To every kindred land beneath the sun;
All honor to our own immortal dead,
Who, through the darkness, on to victory led.
And while sweet violets bloom above their graves,
And while the stars and stripes above them waves,
A nation's blessing shall their requiem be,
Who purchased with their blood, our liberty!

* * * * * *

Ring, ring the tidings, Independence Bell!
To all the nations the glad story tell,—
Liberty! Peace! and Union! all combined,
Around our altars sacredly entwined.
While over all, in stately triumph waves
Our glorious flag,—to kindly welcome all
Who meet as friends in Independence Hall.
Glory to God! for what our fathers wrought;
Glory to God! for what the years have brought.
O, car of Progress, speed in conquest on
Throughout the century about to come.
Heaven guard, and keep our country's honor pure
While earth shall last, and rolling time endure.

MABEL.

Song.

I am thinking to-night of thee, Mabel,
    Mabel, so peerless and fair,
Of the heavenly light in thy violet eyes,
    And the gold of thy rippling hair—
Of the moonlit path where we used to meet
And walk together with stainless feet.

I am wearing a garland for thee, Mabel,
    Pale violets, and roses white;
As pure as the flowers that forever bloom,
    In the gardens of golden light;
They whisper to me, of departed years—
As I moisten their lips with my falling tears.

Why art thou so cruel and cold, Mabel?
    Why spurn me away from thy side?
Sweet Mabel, my love, my angelic queen!
    Tell me this: wilt thou be my bride.
Patiently, fondly, I here shall wait
Until from thy lips I have learned my fate.

Heaven guard and keep thee, Mabel, Mabel!
    When another's home thou shalt bless;
But love, should life's shadows around thee fall,
    Wilt thou think of my soul's distress.
And now, that I journey across the sea,
Wilt thou breathe at the altar a prayer for me?

FADED LILIES.

My lilies, pure white lilies,
   Have all faded from my sight;
Just as many of the loved ones
   I am dreaming of to-night.
With their lustrous waxen petals
   And sweetly-perfumed breath,
I forgot, that like the roses
   They were subject unto death.

I asked the clover blossoms,
   To give the answer true;
Where are my shining lilies?
   I have searched the garden through;
But the clover blossoms answered—
   As they drooped their graceful heads—
"You will find their faded petals
   Scattered o'er the garden beds."

Then I turned away in sadness
   And in sorrow breathed a sigh;
Although I know, while flowers may fade,
   Bright things can never die.
Another year, when summer comes
   My faith shall not be vain;
My silver-throated lilies then
   Shall bloom for me again.

A GIFT OF ROSES.

The flowers you gave me yester-night—
Those roses of crimson and fairy white
As they pour perfume on the morning breeze
They whisper to me of a heart at ease.
      Oh, beautiful roses
        Hasten to twine
      Your tranquil life
        In this soul of mine.

The roses in white and crimson sheen,
Encircled by leaves of golden green,
Have been kissed by the lips of fairies bright
As they whispered their love in the soft moonlight.
      The subtle tints of
        Their leaves disclose
      The blushes that on
        My love's cheeks repose.

No flash of the rubies, nor diamonds' glare
Can with the sweet blush of these buds compare,
Nor delicate pearls from the foaming sea,
With the flowers that my darling gave to me.
      May your life, my love,
        Be as free from care,
      As the rose that so near
        To my heart I wear.

A WELCOME.

[Read by Crypti Palmoni, at the Convention of the Right Worthy Grand Lodge of Good Templars of the World, Washington, D. C., May 28, 1884.]

Hark, the bells of joy are ringing
   And our flags are all unfurled,
While we gather here to welcome
   All the nations of the world;
With a love that is immortal
   And a hope that is sublime,
Proud Columbia's hand is offered
   Unto friends of every clime.

Friends of every land and ocean
   Where the human voice is heard,
Have aroused this great commotion
   And Columbia's pulse is stirred;
For around us is the dawning
   Of a new and glorious light—
"On to glory!" is our watchword
   And our battle flags are bright.

Welcome friends, a thousand welcomes,
   To this grand fraternity!
Welcome from the land of flowers,
From the pure arcadian bowers,
   Where the southern sunset lingers,
And the palm-tree dips its fingers
   In the billows of the sea;

And the southern cross is lighted,
By the lamps which heaven ignited,
   And from where the star of empire
Grandly takes its westward way—
   Loving friends, we give you welcome
And a greeting hand to-day.

Ah, your coming gives us pleasure,
More than poet's song can measure,
   For you answered by your presence
When you heard the bugle call.
   You have come to give us power
   In this great momentous hour,
When the battle wages strongly
   Between purity and sin.
Toiling friends we bid you welcome,
   Welcome, welcome, one and all.
Love inspired we'll march together,
'Mid life's storms or summer weather,
   'Till our husbands and our lovers,
   'Till our fathers, sons and brothers
From the wine cup shall be free!

Though our altar fires burn slowly,
Yet our cause is pure and holy,
   And our noble temperance band
Has been strengthened through the suffering
   Of the women of our land.
Not a soul shall be discouraged,
   Neither faint beside the way

For we've seen a greater struggle
    Than the struggle of to-day.

*   *   *   *   *

We have wept beside our battle-fields,
    We have wept beside our slain!
We wept to see our heroes fall—
    We felt their throbbing pain—
We wept because we loved them
    When we saw them march away;
Noble men whose names emblazon
    Our escutcheon of to-day!

Our heroes fell! but then we heard
    United voices rise;
Shout after shout, throughout the land
    Ascended toward the skies;
And sealed in blood the covenant
    Of glory yet to be,
For the shackles had been broken
    And four million souls were free.

And while we pray that Heaven will spare
    Our land from such a strife;
The men who make our nation's laws
    Must give our nation life.
Full twenty million human souls
    Are pleading here to-day—
"Oh! save us from the tempter's cup
    And open up the way

That leads to honor, love and truth,
   And blessings yet to be,"
And hark! our temperance hosts exclaim;
   "Make way for liberty."
The trumpet voice comes thundering down
   The corridor of years,
Yet gently as an angel's hand
   It wipes away our tears.

Behold, the arch of promise bright;
   Our hosts with proud *eclat*,
Are marching onward in the fight,
   Hurrah, hurrah, hurrah!
On, on to victory, onward on!
   Our flags are all unfurled,
The *reveille* has just begun,
   Our battle-field's the world.

We need not fear, our soldiers brave
   Shall never suffer loss;
For lo, the Crescent reaches forth
   To greet the Southern Cross,
And thus united we shall be
   Through every day and hour,
'Till all our loved ones shall be free
   From Rum's despotic power!

AT LAST.

A Romance.

She loved him not, though her pledge was given
    To love through all the years;
And cheeks once pink with blushes
    Were stained with cruel tears.
Where the sea-foam's eternal splendor
    Lay white, 'neath a moonlit sky,
This beautiful maiden was waiting,
    Hoping only to droop and die.
Across the billows her lover
    Had gone for a year or more;
And she secretly prayed that his vessel
    Would never return to shore.

    *   *   *   *   *

In a low-roofed, vine-bower'd cottage,
    Where the honey-suckle's bloom,
Lifted from scarlet censers,
    Rich volumes of sweet perfume,
This maiden found a new lover,
    Who kissed with a manly grace
Despair from her brow of marble,
    And grief from her tear-stained face;
At last she had found her ideal—

What more could she want beside?
And with lips that out-blushed the roses
   She vowed to become his bride.

   *   *   *   *   *   *

'Twas night—and the tempest's blackness
   Loomed up in a threatening sky—
And above the roar of the waves was heard
   The ominous sea-gull's cry.
The sea, with a wierd unearthly voice,
   Dashed angrily to and fro;
Louder the wail of the breakers—
   As louder the storm-winds blow.
A fisherman ran to the cottage;
   His face of an ashen white;
"Help!" in tremulous tones he shouted,
   "The *Dolphin* is wrecked to-night!"

"The *Dolphin*, oh Heaven;" shrieked the maiden;
   "Heaven send that no ill betide,—
The captain commanding the *Dolphin*,
   I once promised to be his bride.
Go, save him, go save him," she faltered,
   "Now the tale of my life is told;
For I must abandon the new love,
   And give myself up to the old,"
"Give me the life-line; I'll save him!"
   Spoke her lover—my faith shall be true;
"But if I should be lost in the sea to-night,
   Forget not my love for you."

Then he clasped to his heart the maiden
  In a lover's manly embrace,
And pressed a sweet kiss of parting
  On her beautiful upturned face;
And seizing the life-line firmly,
  He plunged in the stormy tide,
And bravely battled the waters
  Till he reached the wrecked *Dolphin's* side.

Then he called to the noble captain—
  So firm and gallant and true—
"Give me the command of the *Dolphin*,
  Your sweetheart is waiting for you.
Take the life-line, strong arms are waiting
  To carry the life-line in;"
Then above the roar of the ocean
  There sounded a crash and a din;
But the captain rescued from the billows
  Was safe on the welcome shore;
While the *Dolphin*,—ah, where was the *Dolphin?*
  'Neath the storm waves to rise no more.

* * * * * *

At length came a time of mourning,
  And a widow, not young, but fair,
Sat dreamily watching the sunlight
  That gleamed in her shining hair;
Here and there a pale thread of silver,
  Was blent with the shimmering gold,

But autumn had made her more lovely
    Than summer, a thousand fold.
Sweet and low was the voice of her sorrow
    As she whispered, "Ah, woe is me,
One sleeps 'neath the grass in the churchyard—
    And one in the treacherous sea."

    *   *   *   *   *   *

Was it the form of an angel
    Appeared at the fair mourner's side?
Was it the voice of the sea she heard,
    As on dashed the incoming tide?
"Cease, darling, O cease thy repining,
    Let me kiss from thy lips those tears;
With a love time has not disenchanted,
    I have waited these twenty years;
That thy love was pure as an angel's,
    I had not a reason to doubt;
When to save from the deep thy first lover,
    I carried the life-line out."

    *   *   *   *   *   *

And now the white sea-foam's splendor
    Is touched with a pencil of gold,
And these lovers, so blest in the new love,
    Will ever remember the old.

OH, NO, NOT THERE.

A vision of beauty, with gossamer wings
And a golden harp with golden strings,
Drew near to my side, as I, worn with care,
   Sat wearily watching the shadows go by,
And dreaming of bliss in my home over there;
I asked the vision if on that side the shore
True peace might be found, and it said—"evermore."

I asked the vision, robed in garments of white,
Do roses fade in the gardens of light,
Or cruel storms beat in the lily's pure face,
   Or the lightning's flash, with pencil of fire,
On the pale sweet brow of the violet, trace
Dark lines of grief, as on this side the shore—
The sweet voice answered, "oh, no, nevermore!"

Then I asked the vision, as it floated along
Trilling musical echoes of silvery song,
In the shining city, do joys ever fade—
   Day change to night, and our smiles to tears,
And our fondest hopes in the dust be laid,
Or wither the blossoms we fondly wear;
Then the sweet voice answered, "oh, no, not there!"

Then I asked the vision whence it came,
And what was its mission, and what its name—
When lo, for an answer, it only smiled—

But it leaned on my breast in a fond caress,
And I knew 'twas the form of my angel child,
And its mission would be, through the coming years,
To soothe my sorrow and dry my tears.

SILVERY WAVES.

[Music arranged by Kimball, published by S. Brainard's Sons.]

Where silvery wavelets flow,
Wavelets flow, wavelets flow;
I'll launch my bark to-night—
Darling come with me.
Beautiful tints of the rich opal sky,
Dreaming upon their fair bosom they lie.

You'll hear the mermaid's song,
Happy song, happy song;
I shall be your gondolier
Safe my boat shall glide.
Sorrow no longer with lingering sway,
Shall from my life take its bright dreams away.

When out on the moonlit sea,
Moonlit sea, moonlit sea;
Give me one smile of love,
Smile of love divine.
Give me the answer my soul longs to hear,
Though you may seal it, my love, with a tear.

AT THE GATE I WAIT FOR THEE.

BELLE MAHONE'S REPLY.

[Music by Mark Havens, published by S. Brainard's Sons.]

At the gate I wait for thee,
Come my loved one, come to me,
Come and wander where the flowers
Fade not in love's rosy bowers,
Where the voice of love is true
As the sky of blue.

CHORUS :—Thy Belle Mahone,
Thy Belle Mahone,
Thine forever, thine forever,
Thy Belle Mahone.

Garlands I will weave for thee,
Blossoms from life's golden tree;
Buds of pure and spotless white
Kissed by Heavenly light.
Weep not darling, I shall wait
For thee at the shining gate,
Loved one weary and alone,
Still thy Belle Mahone.

Heaven without thee would be dark,
Speed thy fairy-phantom bark;

When thy boat shall touch the strand
I shall clasp thy hand
And fondly fold thee to my heart,
No, nevermore again to part,—
God will bring thee safely home
To thy Belle Mahone.

UNDER THE ROOF-TREE.

[Music by Sudds, published by W. F. Shaw.]

Under the roof-tree we gather to-day,
Brothers and sisters from homes far away;
Children are with us, and father is here,
In the old home, in the old home so dear.
Changed is the homestead, but memory is bright,
Bringing back scenes so long faded from sight;
Scenes when we gathered hope's blossoming flowers,
Fresh from the garden of life's morning hours.

Though we are happy, yet still we must weep
For the beloved ones who silently sleep—
Sleep where the marble is chilling and gray—
Oh, precious loved ones, we miss you to-day!
Father stands waiting so near to the shore,
Mother will lovingly welcome him o'er;
Thus comes the question that brings our hearts pain,
Shall we all meet in the old home again?

OUR THANKSGIVING.
November, 1886.

Come, friends and good neighbors, sit down with us here,
While we talk of the blessings that crowned the dead year—
The year that, like others, fled swiftly away,
But bequeathed as a legacy Thanksgiving Day.

Sit close by the fireside before we begin ;
Let the rainstorm without reflect comfort within ;
And, dear friends, please remember, whatever befall,
There is sunshine enough in the world for us all.

To avoid being tiresome the best thing to do
Is to outline the picture that comes in review
In each mind, and be sure that you carefully trace
With the shadows each line of white light in its place.

But do not spare the brush where the shadow must come ;
You will like the work better when thus fairly done—
For so often we find with a tearful surprise,
That the clouds which seemed darkest were nearest the skies.

Now, dear friends, are we thankful in sickness or health—
Quaffing poverty's cup, or the vintage of wealth,
Or sometimes amid plenty, if we should complain,
Do we know that thus living our lives are in vain ?

For another Thanksgiving, we'll set out anew—
And be careful to keep, as an object in view

A record, with day-book and ledger at hand,
That the future may tell how the balance sheets stand.
If your brother is fainting go help him to rise,
Set his feet in the pathway that leads to the skies;
Call the good angels 'round you with voice and with pen;
For the angels of God are the angels of men.
Do your duty whatever your duty may be,
And be thankful for life, 'neath the flag of the free!

FROM THE RILL TO THE OCEAN.

[The author introduces this poem, it being among the first written by her son, Jay Wirt Kail.]

Oh, thou tiny, rippling rill
Coursing down yon distant hill,
Splashing up in silvery spray,
Onward! onward! every day.
Silently you form a brook,
Receiving streams from every nook,
Glittering in the golden light,
You have peace, yet long for might.

Not contented with your sway
Still more turbulent each day,
Thou dost foam and roll and surge
Like some mournful, tuneless dirge.

As a maddened steed you quiver,
Dashing onward to the river,
Where you're swallowed out of sight
Losing freedom, gaining might.

Now, you'll surely be content
And have all your fury spent;
But you've gained the river's motion—
Onward! onward! to the ocean.
Ever dark and restless river
Thou dost plunge and dash and quiver,
Wearing rocks to grains of sand,
That thyself thou mayst expand.

Onward! onward! oh, dark river,
Like an arrow from a quiver,
Like the north wind—shrieking, sighing—
From the mountains thou art flying.
Like a proud steed—madly prancing—
To the end you're wildly dancing;
Pausing not till in the breast
Of the ocean you find rest.

Onward! onward! plunging, rearing;
Swiftly now your home is nearing.
Hark! you hear a great commotion—
"Tis the moaning, storm-tossed ocean.
Vainly now would you return
Since the ocean you discern.
Onward! onward! naught can save
The river buried 'neath the wave.

Thus the peaceful rill grew sad,
And the shining brook grew mad,
For the river's ceaseless motion
Longed and pined to reach the ocean.
But at last they've reached the sea—
They who once were light and free
Now are slaves to power and fame:
Nothing left them save a name.

LINES IN A YOUNG LADY'S ALBUM.

Young friend this world to you must be
    All garlanded with roses,
While shining pearls so fair to see
    Each passing day discloses;
For you, the thrushes sing their song
    With strange artistic power,
And blessings which to few belong
    Crown every day and hour.

But, ah, should clouds across your sky
    Obscure the gathered sweetness—
The rainbow arch of heaven is nigh
    With all its grand completeness;
And tears—so like the summer rain
    That soothes the weeping flowers—
Are given to calm our souls from pain,
    And bless this world of ours.

VIOLETS.

To a Friend.

I walked out in the open fields to-day
To while from care a lonely hour away,
And read a page from nature's open book,
And gather violets blooming by the brook.
The violets started up with mute surprise
While tears of sweetness gathered in their eyes.

I asked the precious violets why those tears,
Does life to you bring recompense of fears?
It seems to me life should be ever sweet
To flowers endowed with beauty so complete.
The brook beside you sings a happy song
As o'er its lowly bed it floats along.

The violets pointed up toward the skies —
A deeper blue reflected in their eyes —
The sun had kissed the tears of night away
And opened up to them a perfect day.
The brooklet whispered low a sweet refrain,
Then danced across the meadow-land again.

Thus, while we walk in life's sequestered way
We meet with human violets every day;
Their fond hearts aching with a withering blight,
Their eyes o'erflowing with the tears of night.

But when through faith they look toward the skies,
The tears of sorrow vanish from their eyes.

To you, dear friend, life is a summer day;
When trials come love kisses them away;
You have not suffered sorrow's wild unrest;
God wills it so, and what He does is best.

CLARIBEL LEE.

[Music by Mark Havens, published by S. Brainard's Sons.]

Breathe softly ye night winds and whisper,
    As ye float o'er the dim distant sea;
Go bear on your light wings a message
    For my darling, sweet Claribel Lee,
Go tell her my heart is so lonely—
The world seems a dark grave to me,
And though sweet be the music, it charms not,
    In the absence of Claribel Lee.

There's no charm for the heart that is breaking,
    Nor beauty in flower or tree;
The robin in vain sings to soothe me—
    While I mourn for my Claribel Lee.
My bark is approaching the river,
    When my heart, prisoned now, shall be free;
Then I'll soar on the wings of the morning
    To the home of my Claribel Lee.

They told me, my darling was dying,
    And they folded her hands on her breast,
Then I knew, tho' they said she was sleeping,
    That my Claribel Lee was at rest.
A smile o'er her brow floated sweetly,
    Holy smile ! it was only for me;
And through life shall the memory linger
    Of the smile of my Claribel Lee.

CHORUS.

I know that my angel is waiting,
    That above she is waiting for me ;
Where the roses immortal are blooming
    At the feet of my Claribel Lee.

THE PAUPER.

I stand upon the grand seashore,
    And view the rocks and drifts of sand ;
The deep waves plashing o'er and o'er,
    Seem like a voice from spirit-land ;
And sea-weeds bow their drooping heads,
    And dip their fingers in the sea,
While reaching down its golden threads,
    The sunlight weaves a crown for me.

A magic harp of thousand strings
    Is waked to life by angel hands ;

A choir seraphic, sweetly sings
   The music of immortal lands;
Beneath the azure-tinted sky,
   Old ocean moans a low refrain,
While white-winged beings from on high
   Re-echo back the song again.

Why comes to me a dream like this—
   To me, a pauper, old and poor?
While life, to some, brings perfect bliss,
   I beg my bread from door to door;
Scorned and upbraided, cast aside—
   No friend to wipe my tears away;
None fear to wound my helpless pride,
   A wanderer by night and day.

Oft in the blessed Book I read
   That mercy, hope and love are free;
And yet I fear, while here I plead,
   There is no hope for such as me;
Doomed! I am doomed to suffer pain;
   Father of all, thine arm make bare,
While here I bow and call Thy name,
   Remove this withering cup of care.

If I could sleep beneath the sea,
   The sea-weed blooming o'er my breast,
Where no false dreams could come to me,
   To mar the sweetness of my rest.

E'en such a fate were better far
  Than life with all its blessings flown,
For then, perchance, some radiant star
  Would watch beside the dead unknown.

OH, SING FOR ME A SONG TO-NIGHT.

SONG.

Oh, sing for me a song to-night,
  A happy song of the olden time;
Your hand so pure and fair my love
  Can touch the keys with a power divine;
My darling, sing a song for me,
A plaintive, touching melody.

Oh, sing for me a song to-night
  With brightness in the mystic flow;
With memories sweet of summer days
  That breathed their fragrance long ago.
Then smile not though I shed a tear
O'er scenes that seem to me so near.

Oh, sing for me a song to-night,
  One precious song, my lady fair,
Of years when life and hopes were gay,
  As flowers that nestle in your hair;
Untasted then, life's wintry stream,
The hours were all a passing dream.

BY AND BY THE ROSES WITHER.

[Music by R. Goerdeler, published by S. Brainard's Sons.]

By and by the roses wither,
    By and by the leaves with fall,
By and by the crimson autumn
    Sheds its lustre over all;
By and by our hopes will brighten,
    Though the swallows homeward fly,
And false friends who seem to love us
    May forget us by and by.

By and by the rose that withers
    Shall uplift its drooping head,
Awakened from its slumbers
    By an angel's gentle tread;
By and by fond hearts be broken
    That have never known a sigh;
Friendless ones with joy will lighten
    In the coming by and by.

By and by there will be false hearts,
    By and by there will be true;
Do I hear you say you doubt it,
    If you do, then, why do you?
By and by bright eyes will moisten
    When beneath the turf we lie—
There will still be those who love us,
    In the silent by and by.

AT CLOSE OF DAY.

Above the towering snow-crowned hills,
   I lift my enraptured eyes ;
For angel hands are painting there
   Heaven's drapery on the skies.

The sun has waved a proud farewell,
   And bowed his golden crown ;
It seems to me that angel arms
   From heaven are reaching down.

The river silently and slow
   Is drifting to the sea ;
A holy calm, like spirit rest,
   Is brooding over me.

How strangely sweet the silence falls
   O'er field and wooded hill ;
No spoken words of gifted tongue,
   Could thus my being fill.

Bright thoughts and beautiful appear,
   My soul is all aglow ;
I heed not wail of winter winds,
   Nor touch of winter's snow.

Thus, when the day of life is done
   And death's pale mystery here,
The soul that trusts the Master's love
   Shall neither faint nor fear.

No poet's words can paint the scene
    That waits our enraptured eyes
When angel hands shall open wide
    The gates of Paradise!

I WAS WAITING FOR A LETTER.

Song.

I was waiting for a letter;
    And the postman seemed so slow,
When I'd hear his coming footsteps
    To some other house h'd go.
When I saw the postman passing
    Then the tears would fill my eyes—
For that I should thus be waiting,
    Gave my heart a sad surprise.

CHORUS.—Repeat four last lines.

While I waited for my letter,
    Ah, the days became so long,
For my soul had lost its brightness,
    And my lips forgot their song;
Even the flowers could breathe no fragrance
    Or no kiss of joy for me,
While I waited for a letter
    From my lover o'er the sea.—CHORUS.

I had waited for my letter
　Till I thought my hopes were vain;
But to-day I saw a loving face
　That soothed my heart of pain;
And a voice—'twas not the postman's—
　Said, "we've just returned from sea,
And, thank Heaven, I find my darling
　Is still waiting here for me."

CHORUS.

O! to-day I got my letter,
　And my soul is full of song,
And I wonder that I ever thought
　The summer days were long.

I'M DREAMING I'M AN INFANT.

[Music by Karl Merz.　Published by S. Brainard's Sons.]

I'm dreaming I'm an infant
　Lulled upon my mother's breast—
Mother's bending sweetly o'er me
　And soothing me to rest.
In prayer I hear her breathing,
　Father take this child of mine,
Fit it for the joys of heaven—
　Oh! make it wholly thine.

I am dreaming, I am dreaming,
   Of childhood's happy hour,
When I watched the laughing sunbeam
   Kiss the dew from off the flower;
I am dreaming of the lilies
   Down at the river side—
Of the pearls that slept beneath them
   Washed by the surging tide.

I am dreaming of the churchyard
   Where the waving willow weeps;
Of the mound beneath its branches
   Where my gentle mother sleeps;
The granite in its grandeur
   In my waking dreams I see,
And I know though mother's sleeping
   She is watching over me.

I am dreaming of the diamonds
   In life's enamelled chain,
Of the pearls I clasped so fondly
   That I ne'er shall clasp again;
Of the jewels in hope's casket,
   That from my grasp have fled;
I'll not pursue them farther—
   Earth's brightest hopes are dead.

I am dreaming now of heaven,
   Of the crowns that angels wear,

And I see the hopes that perished here
  Forever centered there;
And the pearls I lost are gleaming
  On the bright eternal hill,
And mother whispers softly—
  Dearest child I love you still.

MY MOTHER'S FLOWERS.

Song.

I'm walking in the garden paths
  To breathe the evening air;
I've laid aside my daily toil
  My sorrow and my care.
Around me gathered are my friends,
  To guile the lonely hours—
'Twas mother's hand that planted them,
  Oh, how I love these flowers.

My mother dear has gone to rest,
  Her smile no more I see;
But when I look upon her flowers,
  Through them she smiles on me,
I feel her hand upon my head,
  Her kiss upon my brow—
Oh! I am safe from worldly care,
  For mother's with me now.

Again I lisp my evening prayer
   Before I go to sleep;
"If I should die before I wake
   Pray Lord my soul to keep."
Then softly on my trundle-bed
   In angel arms I lay,
And the sweet words, "child go to sleep,"
   I hear my mother say.

Now on the far immortal shore,
   She weaves a garland fair,
And tells me if I follow her
   I may that garland wear;
And though like all terrestrial things
   I soon must pass away,
My mother's flowers my path shall cheer
   Through every toiling day.

TELL ME, DARLING, THAT YOU MISS ME.

Song.

Tell me, darling, that you miss me
   Where the evening shadows fall;
Where the splendor of the autumn
   Sheds its sweetness over all.
When the purple light is fading
   From the western sky away,
And the lamps of heaven are lighted
   At the closing of day.

Tell me, darling, you are waiting
    For the coming of my feet;
That when absent, life is dreary,
    And its dreaming incomplete;
That no lingering voice of summer,
    Nor the autumn's crimson bloom,
Can awake sweet chords of pleasure
    Nor your heart to love attune.

O ye night winds, bear a message
    O'er the proudly rolling sea;
Words of love as yet unspoken—
    Kindly whisper them to me;
Tell me that my love is waiting—
    Of the fairest the most fair,
Where the autumn tints are fading
    She is waiting for me there.

I'LL DREAM LOVE OF THEE.

Song.

I'm dreaming, my darling—
    I'm dreaming of thee,
When sleeping or waking,
    By land or by sea;
Should darkness and sorrow
    Through life come to me,
To brighten the shadows,
    I'll dream love of thee.

As a bird of the spring-time
   Conceals in her breast,
When soaring away to
   Her leaf-hidden nest,
The song that so sweetly
   She sings from the tree,
I dream of my darling—
   I dream love of thee.

Sometimes in my dreaming,
   Beside thee I stand,
I feel the soft touch of
   Your lily-pure hand;
And glory surpassing
   The blue of the skies
Illumines my soul from
   Your heavenly eyes.

And thus while your kisses
   Are tender and sweet,
With passionate pleading
   I bow at thy feet;
The answer of fate that
   Your lips would conceal,
Your smiles and your blushes
   Can only reveal.

In some fairy bower,
   In sweet summer-time,
I know I shall claim thee
   Forever as mine,

Till then, through life toiling
  My pleasure shall be
To dream of my darling—
  To dream love of thee.

JENNIE VERNON.

[Jennie Vernon, a beautiful child, whose father was killed in battle, presented Col. Lansing a garland of flowers with the request that they be placed on a rebel soldier's grave.]

Day was drawing near its close,
  Lilies and violets going to sleep ;
The robin was singing her vesper hymn,
  When I heard the patter of fairy feet ;
I saw 'twas a child divinely fair
  With deep blue eyes so sweet and mild ;
But precious, sacred, holy tears
  Dimmed the eyes of the fairy child.

She seemed an angel sent from Heaven
  With a balm to sooth each aching heart,
To cool the fevered scorching brain
  And words of truth and life impart.
To banish all coroding cares
  And soothe the suffering mourner's tears ;
To link in love's immortal chain,
  Our souls, and brighten all the years.

She held aloft a garland fair,
    Just gathered from an odorous dell,
Where dew-drops kiss the blushing leaves
    And evening zephyrs their music tell.
She spoke—I paused entranced to hear—
    "Lay this wreath on a rebel soldier's grave,
I love them all, my father sleeps
    Where orange blossoms o'er him wave.

Perhaps some child of the sunny south
    Will drop on father's grave a tear,
Or plant a flower to mark the spot
    Where lies the form to me so dear."
Oh Father! let thy will be done,
    Let childhood's lips perfect thy praise;
Oh, light of Heaven, illume our souls—
    Speed on the bright and happy days.

When bound by friendship's golden chain,
    A band of brothers we shall be;
When malice crushed to earth shall die
    And freedom's flag float o'er the free.
Then we shall blend with kindred lights,
    Who've passed before to Heaven above,
And breathe a soul refreshing air
    Perfumed by censers filled with love.

SUMMER NIGHT.

Oh, summer night, divinely bright,
Resting in Luna's silver light;
While by her side, one glittering star
Directs my wandering thoughts afar.

Thy shadows steal and hopes reveal
Which only trusting souls can feel;
While worshipping before thy shrine;
Oh make these joys forever mine.

In evening hours, thy sylvan showers,
Fall as the dew upon the flowers;
While o'er the shadowy wildwood dell,
Soft falls the notes of vesper bell.

Around my feet pale violets sleep;
With loving hearts the roses weep,
And greet me with a fond caress
While blessing with their tenderness.

Oh, summer night, with radiant light
The dewdrops showering crystals bright,
And fire-flies flitting through the glade
Dispense at once both light and shade.

Sweet summer night, so fair and bright,
Encircling me with holy light.
Thy smiles, my darkest hour can cheer—
Joy reigns supreme when thou art near.

THE MUSIC OF TEARS.

The wind hath a low, sad voice, to-night,
   As I dream of departed years;
The wail of the breeze, as it floats thro' the trees,
   Is the mystical music of tears.
Each echoing throb, like the heart-felt sob
   Of a soul over-burdened with grief,
That can only find, to the wearied mind,
   In the music of tears, relief.

The wind hath a tender voice, to-night,
   As it sweeps over last year's leaves,
All covered with snow, and it whispers low,
   Of the grain and the golden sheaves
That will soon appear, for the harvest year
   Is dawning all over our land;
When the silver light of the sickle bright
   Shall gleam in the reaper's hand.

Oh! the wonderful keys of the wind, to-night,
   Are touched by a master hand,
And the plaint refrain is echoed again
   By a melody deep and grand;
And the silvery song as it floats along,
   Giveth hope for the coming years;
For the roseate glory of smiling morn
Of the gloom and the darkness of night is born,
   I have heard thro' the music of tears.

SEND ME.

Hymn.

The harvest work is truly great,
   Though laborers are few;
Yet all who have a will to work
   Can find a work to do.
Oh, give me then some humble place,
   Thy love my guide shall be,
And where the path of duty leads,
   My Father, pray send me!

I would not from the mountain-top
   Look down upon the vale;
For should I strive the hill to climb,
   E'en there my strength might fail;
But I would launch my fragile bark
   Out on life's stormy sea,
And ask of Him who rules the storm,
   My Father, pray send me!

Oh, may my life show forth Thy praise
   Each day and every hour;
Oh, give me grace to trust my all
   To Heaven's almighty power!
Though sorrows compass me about,
   My soul shall cling to Thee;
And plead from out the gathering storm,
   My Father, pray send me!

I AM WEARY, OH, MY FATHER.

Hymn.

I am weary, oh, my Father,
  My Father I would rest;
Oh, let me lean my aching head,
  Upon Thy loving breast.
Surrounded by temptation,
  By trial and by pain,
I only can be comforted
  By trusting in Thy name.

This world is very beautiful,
  E'en here, the angels sing;
They tell us of our Father's love
  The happy tidings bring,—
But death is here, and steals away
  The dearest and the best;
The polished marble marks the spot
  Where our beloved ones rest.

The rose, in all its conscious pride,
  Is circled by its thorns—
'Tis thus the sunshine of our lives
  Is shaded by life's storms.
But when we lean upon Thy breast
  We see the golden light,
And clouds sometimes so threatening
  Descend in blessings bright.

SOFTLY AND LOW.

Softly and low good angels weep,
Guarding o'er those, who silent sleep;
Softly the gentle whisperings come:
Pilgrim, oh, hasten to thy home.

Softly and low red roses bloom,
Shedding their fragrance o'er the tomb;
Then tenderly blushing they pass away,
Short lived beauties of a day.

Softly and low life's dream is told,
Through unseen chords on harps of gold
While hidden fingers sweep the strings
Our heart the answering echo sings.

Softly and low at evening floats,
Over the Alpine hills, sweet notes;
Labor all ended and sins confessed,
Weary, the shepherds go home to rest.

Softly and low the years go by—
Yet who can tell from whence they fly?
This we do know, that they leave their trace
Of hope and sorrow on every face.

TO MY BRIDE OF THIRTY YEARS.

To Mr. and Mrs. V. P. W.

With friends and children we have met,
  Around the ingleside,
To celebrate the happy day
  When you became my bride.
Oh! can it be that thirty years
  Have with their blessing fled?
And can it be that friends we loved,
  Are numbered with the dead?

It seems to me but yesterday
  Since you were young and fair;
Your cheeks were pink as apple bloom
  'Mid springtime's fragrant air.
I loved you then, I love you still,
  My heart is yours alone—
For through the years your smile has **blest**
  And sanctified our home.

My thoughts go back and life appears
  A fitful summer dream;
How strange that we have glided down
  So far along life's stream.
And yet our Father's loving hand
  Has led us on aright;
With just enough of sorrow's clouds
  To make life's sunshine bright.

While we beside the festal board
  Our loving vows renew,
We'll ask for grace to make us strong
  To walk life's journey through.
Though autumn winds have strewn our path
  With summer's faded leaves,
The golden grain of harvest time
  Is gathered with the sheaves.

We know not what the years may bring,
  But this we understand :
Beyond the sea of life appears
  The blissful summer land,
Where spring-time blossoms never fade,
  Nor summer flowers decay ;
There angel hands shall open wide
  The gates of perfect day.

WHAT SHALL WE NAME THE BABY?

What shall we name the baby?
  Our darling and our pride ;
With pink hands softly folded
  She nestles by our side.
Violet, because the violet's blue
Speaketh the language, "ever true."

Or shall we name her Llily,
   This precious babe of ours—
We always call the lily .
   The fairest of the flowers—
Its shining petals speak to me
The noble language, purity.

Then we might name her Daisy;
   For in the early spring
The daisy wakes from pleasant dreams
   To hear the robin sing,
And speaks from out its laughing eyes,
" True beauty never, never dies."

Then Snowdrop would be pretty;
   * For with a gentle grace,
Carnation and the snowdrop
   Are blended in her face.
To it the language has been given,
"Forget-me-not," and "thoughts of heaven."

But why not call her Pansy?
   The pansy's purple hair,
Is crowned by a rich jewel
   Such as a queen might wear.
Its language shall our darling's be—
" Sweet be thy dreams and dream of me."

Or Rosebud—though soon withered,
   We may not call them dead;

When their pure leaves are faded,
  They sweetest incense shed.
Of virtues, roses speak of three—
"Love, innocence and constancy."

God bless our baby blossom!
  Angels of peace and love
Guard o'er our priceless treasure,
  Good angels from above.
We know when life's brief dream is past,
Our flower shall bloom in heaven at last.

GLOOMY WEATHER.

Oh, dark, dull days,—
  No summer sunshine dancing
Across the fields
  To music soul-entrancing.
The robin folds
  His wings of painted glory;
The dove has ceased
  To tell her plaintive story.

Fair flowers of June
  Have lost their magic sweetness;
And trees bow down
  Their drapery of completeness.

All nature mourns,—
  For skies are dull with weeping;
Its blue eyes closed
  The meadow violet's sleeping.

Though June may wear
  Her bridal veil in sorrow,
Nature gives hope
  For brightness on the morrow.
By faith we learn—
  The hidden source divining—
That far beyond the gloom,
  Heaven's light is shining.

AN AUTUMN REVERY.

Oh, thou royal autumn day,
Drifting from my sight away,
While your banners blue and gold,
Draped with crimson in each fold,
Seem to say as you pass by,—
Earth recedes, but heaven is nigh,
And with sunlight dropping low
Earth and heaven are aglow.

Nature's harps are all in tune,
Just as when the leafy June

Came, all garlanded with flowers
Gathered from the woodland bowers;
When her violet covered feet
Lightly danced, where roses sweet
Softly blushed, with new-born grace,
At the summer queen's embrace.

Now the Hallow-e'en is nigh.
When the maiden, with a sigh,
Asks the book of fate unrolled
Will her destiny be told;
Will her lover, brave and true,
Look through eyes of brown or blue;
Will the voice of coming years
Bring her smiles, or bring her tears.

Ah, sweet maiden, for your fate
On life's threshold do not wait;
But from all life's budding flowers
Gather strength for later hours;
For the joy that blooms to-day
May to-morrow fade away; .
But through life remember this,
Heaven is love, and love is bliss.

COLD, MY DARLING.

Cold, my darling, lie the shadows
   Out upon the snow-robed lea,
And the wind with mournful music
   Sweeps in grandeur from the sea.
Cold, so cold the darkening shadows
   Where the wreaths of autumn lay,
And the pretty blue-eyed violet
   Sweetly breathed its life away.

Cold my darling, cold and quiet;
   Silent is the robin's trill;
Nature shows no sign of gladness—
   Even the brooklet's voice is still.
Trust me, darling, though the shadows
   Deepen on life's stormy sea,
For I know glad days of brightness
   Wait my love for you and me.

Joy! the glorious dawn is breaking,
   See the red light in the skies,
And the golden day reflected
   In the splendor of your eyes.
Cold, my darling—never, never
   Love's sweet flower that blooms for you;
And though dreams of joy may perish
   Still believe me ever true.

GIVE ME BACK MY CHILDHOOD.

Give me back my childhood's
  Sunshine and its shade;
Let me romp again
  'Mid the flowers of the glade;
Let me gather garlands—
  Roses bright and fair—
Twine the scarlet maple leaves
  In my shining hair.

Take me to the valley
  Where the violets sleep;
Let me kiss the tears from
  The lilies when they weep;
Let me watch the primrose
  Smile with dreaming eyes,
When the stars of evening
  Wake with sweet surprise.

Give me back my childhood—
  Life's immortal day!
When the glory of a flower
  Smooths life's cares away;
When each chord of music
  Wakes a sweet refrain.
Ah, can it be we may not know
  Such days of joy again.

LIFE IS SHORT AND DEATH IS NEAR.

Life is short and death is near,
   Lo, the golden moments flying,
Whisper as they disappear,
   Passing hours are swiftly dying.
Whisper, as they float along,
   Crowned with summer's royal sweetness,
Hearken to our trembling song—
   Years, are days, in full completeness.

Days o'erclouded by the night,
   Days of woe, and days of sorrow,
Days without a sunbeam bright,
   Hopeless for the coming morrow;
Days when hearts were bending low,
   Weary with their weight of weeping;
Cheeks were pale as drifted snow
   'Neath the storms of winter sleeping.

Days that brought a tranquil joy,
   And the weary heart grew lighter;
Days that knew not pain's alloy—
   Heaven was near and earth was brighter.
Days made pure by deeds of love,
   And we knew that God intended
Thus to lift our souls above,
   When the days of toil are ended.

Life is short and death is near,
    Labor for the Master's reaping;
Soon the harvest shall appear—
    Let no soul be idly sleeping,
Soon the Saviour's voice shall say
    Unto thee a crown is given;
Welcome to the gates of day,
    Welcome to a home in heaven.

IN THE GARDEN.

One day in my garden I found a blush rose,
    All bright with the dew of the sky,
And while gently I saw its soft petals unclose,
    Then I knew that the summer was nigh.

But at noontime my rose bowed its beautiful head,
    For the sun had been strong and severe—
And at even from its bosom the petals had fled
    And its fond heart was moist with a tear.

But around me there floated a fragrance so sweet,
    As the rose sighed away its last breath;
Then I knew that in glory its life was complete,
    While it passed through the shadow of death.

Like the rose from my garden our lives pass away,
    And the work of our destiny's done;
But beyond the blue arch of heaven's glorified day,
    Our lives shall be truly begun.

INTO THE FIELDS WITH GOLDEN GRAIN.

Into the fields with golden grain,
   A sower went one day to sow;
He scattered wheat, that sun and rain
   Might help the fruitful germs to grow.
Then he prayed that the Lord of the harvest would come
And bless the good work his hands had done.

Some of the precious golden seed
   Fell on the dusty barren way,
And fowls of the air, in their hungry need,
   Came and bore the good seed away.
And with anguish deep and sorrowing pain
The sower wept that his work was vain.

Some of the grains of wheat had found
   Beneath the sun's o'erpowering ray,
Root where the rocks and stones abound,
   And they withered at close of day.
Then the sower wept in his deep despair,
To find that at harvest no wheat was there.

Seed that was sown amid blossoming flowers,
   Grew in the crimson morning light;
But weeds came up in a few short hours
   And hid the good wheat from his sight.
Then the sower exclaimed that his work was vain,—
But he toiled and trusted the Master's name.

After the passing of many years—
  Behold! a rich harvest of golden wheat;
Then the sower knew—though he sowed in tears,
  That his work was now all complete.
Thus shall the harvest of life be well,
  If we work and wait—as the years will tell.

BITTER WINE.

In youth I dreamed a dream, 'twas wondrous fair;
Around me flowers were blooming everywhere,
And roseate clouds sailed slowly in the sky,
Their glowing banners floating from on high.

A river, dancing on from day to day,
Entwined the shore with wreaths of crystal spray,
While floating out their white wings overhead
To catch the perfumed breeze broad sails were spread.

Birds sang sweet songs and each ecstatic trill
Awoke sweet chords that made my being thrill;
I asked my heart amid the enchanting bliss—
If heaven could be a happier place than this.

The world seemed pure, I little understood
That but for selfish ends the world is good.
Thus in my dream, so strangely incomplete,
I pressed life's roses—smiling at my feet.

When my long cherished dream dissolved away
I woke to find my idols were but clay;
In vain I asked of my deluded mind,
Where are the joys which now I cannot find?

Ah, would that I had earlier learned to know
That bitter wine must in life's chalice flow.
Though rich the promise of the vintage time,
Some unripe clusters bring forth bitter-wine.

Then press with willing lips life's mystic bowl;
The bitter wine makes strong the fainting soul.
Life is a problem, which when understood
Reveals alike the evil and the good.

CAST OFF.

I saw her in her bridal robes,
    The shimmering lace adorning;
She knew not that mad love for him
    Within my soul was burning.
She dreamed not, that to my proud lips
    Love's chalice he presented,
And though I dashed the wine away,
    I ever had repented.

I thought, that he would come again,
   His wealth of love revealing,
And I would deign to smile on him
   My own deep love concealing.
He only said, "the wound to heal
   Shall be my life's endeavor;
Remember, if we part to-night,
   That it shall be forever."

Long years had passed, he did not come;
   One evening by the river—
I met a noble manly form:
   It was my absent lover.
No words of tenderness he spoke
   To show a heart relenting;
Though on my knees I wildly told
   Him, of my soul's repenting.

"You are too late," he coldly said,
   "The truth I will not smother;
The love, that might have once been thine,
   Is given to another."
Now, at my feet the arrows fall
   From hope's immortal quiver—
Unloved, unsought, ah, woe is me,
   I am cast off forever.

THEN LIFE WERE WORTH THE LIVING.

Although my tasks are hard to bear,
  Yet I am often singing
The merry chimes of rythmic song
  That in my soul are ringing;
And while each day new duty brings,
  Within my soul is stealing
A voice, to wake the sleeping chords
  Of deep poetic feeling.

I wonder why my life is blest
  By such enchanting sweetness—
For wealth, or fame, could never bring
  Such gems of rare completeness;
And yet, sometimes, I fain would sigh
  And stoop to weak repining;
Poor foolish heart, too blind to see
  The glory round me shining.

While thus I mused, and thus I toiled,
  Throughout the passing hours;
I went one day, that I might hold
  Sweet converse with the flowers.

White clouds were sailing in the sky;
  A robin's voice was singing;
A cypress on the garden path
  Its scarlet bells was flinging.

Ah, stately cypress—thus I said—
   Bright queen of floral beauty;
A lesson I have learned of you;
   A sermon on life's duty.

I see your queenly head is crowned
   With summer's royal splendor,
And yet with all your stately life
   Your heart is pure and tender.
There's not a daisy at your feet
   Too low for your caressing;
To each you cast a shining crown
   And give it with your blessing.

And this—methinks I hear you say
   Though soon my life must perish,
I care not, if the humblest flower
   One act of mine shall cherish;
One little deed of kindness done
   With pure, unselfish giving;
One mourner blest, one heart made glad,
   Then life were worth the living.

ONLY A WOMAN'S SMILE.

Only a woman's smile—did I say—
   But my heart with its throbbing pain
Grows light as the balmy breeze that floats,
   And memory is young again.
Before me sweet visions of beauty rise,
   And forgotten is my despair—
While the holy light of a woman's smile
   Is blended with all my care.

Only a woman's smile—but the stars
   Bow down their golden heads,
To listen to woman's magic voice,
   And to kiss the earth she treads.
The world would be only a dreary waste—
   A sad, unbroken wild—
No light, no love, no joy, no hope
   Had woman never smiled.

Only a woman's smile—but it lives
   Through all the long dead years;
For there's nothing can equal a woman's smile
   Save only a woman's tears.
Woman can make the most humble home
   As bright as the portals of heaven;
The comforting power to bless human hearts
   Unto woman's charmed life has been given.

OUR ANGEL WATCHERS.

Our dear departed loved ones
  Oh, are they ever near,
To touch the throbbing chords of love
  And see the falling tear.
Do they whisper of a better home
  Beyond this world of pain;
Do they gently, oh so gently
  Fold us in their arms again.

Do we think, because we laid them
  'Neath the violets down to sleep;
Where roses of the summer-time
  Their tears of sadness weep;
And though, that we in vain must wait
  Their coming at the door—
Do we think that we shall never see
  Our angel watchers more.

They are chanting; they are chanting
  Happy songs of love divine—
Oh, I often hear the voices
  Of those precious friends of mine;
The echo of the music
  Floats across the distant stream,
I hear it in my waking hours
  And hear it when I dream.

And when my heart is lonely,
    And for a balm would seek,
My precious angel watchers
    Fond words of comfort speak.
And then my soul takes courage
    As o'er my senses thrill
Such words of blissful melody
    As only they can trill.

ANOTHER YEAR.

My roses failed to bloom for me this year,
In vain I waited their unfolding charms;
Vile worms with traitorous hearts destroyed the leaves
Of the fair buds smiling beneath the eaves,
And lifting at blissful, holy hour of prayer
Their incense sweet upon the evening air.
Ah, they may smile again, my heart to cheer
Another year, in joy another year.

My pansies, children of most loving care,
Their bright eyes sparkling with the morning dew,
The sweet expression of each beaming face,
The birthplace of a more exquisite grace;
In them I hoped my joy would be complete,
But found them withered blossoms at my feet,
The jewels faded in their purple hair.
Yet, they may bless my life another year.

I built a ship and sent it out to sea,
Freighted with deeds of kindness for the friends I love;
Some cruel light-house with its glittering ray
Allured my gilded bark from me away—
Its precious cargo hidden out of sight,
My deeds of kindness all are unrequite.
Another year my ship may sail for me;
Another year, ah yes, another year.

Hope's wing is broken, but it is not dead—
Trusting, it soars aloft to realms above,
And hope that faded with departed years
Shall rise immortal—though it be in tears.
For ah, perchance, false friends may yet be true,
All this, even more, another year may do.
For me life's ripening harvest shall be sweet,
Though seeds my hands have sown seem incomplete.
'Tis winter now, but summer-time is near,
With golden fruitage of another year.

THRICE WEDDED.

I am dreaming of my darling,
    And the days that long are past,
Sever not the blissful seeming—
    All too bright and pure to last;

For the long forgotten memories
   Into deathless blossoms grow—
As before me floats the vision
   Of my love of long ago.

Softly breathe, O blushing roses,—
   Hold your breath of fragrance sweet,
Lest your breathing wake my slumber
   And my dream be incomplete.
Cease your warbling, robin-redbreast;
   Thrushes chant your matins low,
Let me hear the old, old story
   From my love of long ago.

In the rosy hours of spring-time
   I had given her my heart,
But a fate both stern and cruel
   Bade our paths lie far apart.
Only in the great hereafter
   I may learn why this was so—
Why, through life I have been parted
   From my love of long ago.

Though three times I have been wedded,
   And each time I thought my wife
Was the best of noble women,
   And the glory of my life.
Though my eyes have lost their brightness,
   And my head is crowned with snow,
Yet I never have forgotten,
   My beloved of long ago.

BRIGHTNESS.

The world is full of beauty,
   Of gold and crimson light;
Break not the blissful dreaming
   That charms my soul to-night.
My heart is wildly throbbing
   With joy, akin to pain—
Spare me; break not the mystic spell,
   Oh, sever not the chain.

Dance on, oh rippling waters
   Across the rock-bound strand;
Laugh at the poisoned chalice
   That grief holds in her hand;
I'll take from joy the gilded cup
   And quaff the sparkling wine,
Fresh from the purple clusters
   Just gathered from the vine.

'Twas pain, the soul refiner,
   That brought this perfect bliss;
My brightest dreams of pleasure
   Have never equalled this.
Earth's withering cares and sorrows
   Have vanished from my view;
Heaven's gates of pearl are open
   And the splendor shining through.

SUBMISSION.

I would that I could soar away
Up through the straight and narrow way,
And enter the blissful realms of day,
   Where thought has often flown.
My soul aflame with holy fire,
I'd touch with joy some angel's lyre,
And as the strains rose higher, higher,
   I'd bow before the throne.

But ah, were life a summer dream;
If no dark cloud should intervene,
And joys were lasting as they seem,
   Would my poor selfish heart
Deal gently with a brother's woe;
Lift burdens from the poor and low;
With sweet words soothe the mourner's woe
   And of it bear a part?

With patience I must learn to wait,
But not with those who come too late,
To enter at the golden gate
   Celestial joys on high.
I'll follow at the Saviour's feet,
And pray my work shall be complete,
Each duty through His love made sweet;
   Thus Heaven is ever nigh.

DEPARTED JUNE.

Flower-crowned May went to sleep near a musical rill,
Just when June was beginning her songs to trill,—
Went to sleep 'neath the silvery moon.
   June's cheeks grew red
   And she blushingly said
    I'll scatter fresh flowers
   O'er the sleeper's bed—
Then sweet bloomed the roses of June.

June followed her sleeping sister May,
And the flowers wept when she went away,—
And the dove wailed a mournful tune.
   But blithe and gay
   Was our queen that day;
    As little children
   When at their play.
Light-hearted and happy June.

She will come again with her smiles and tears,
When the cycles pass of departing years;
She will come in her beauty and bloom.
   With blossoms rare
   In her golden hair;
    Clothed in wonderful robes
   Such as summer shall wear,
Then we'll welcome our smiling June.

WITH THE GIFT OF A ROSE.

You gave me a rose, my fair young friend—
    A rose all fresh with morning dew—
A fragrant rose, whose blushes blend
    With the smile on your lips, so pure and true.
A radiant rose you seem to me,
With joyful heart and fancy free,
And dancing feet that gayly glide
O'er life's summer sea, with its rising tide.

O sweet-breathed rose! O precious flower!
    In silent language all your own
You speak of dell and woodland bower
    Where wood-nymphs weave their leafy throne.
Where thrushes join in gleeful song,
While echoing hills the notes prolong,
And rippling streams with music sweet
Go dancing on with fairy feet.

The artist's pencil seeks in vain
    To paint the glory of a rose;
The poet's soul must throb with pain,
    And dream in love's secure repose,
Ere he can sing a tender song
Of memories dear that round him throng,
Of roses sweet; that faded soon
But—blest the summer with their bloom.

My fair young friend, your gift shall be
   Remembered in the future years,
Though life should only bring to me
   A gathered recompense of tears.
Ah, may your life be bright with leaves
All harvested in golden sheaves,
And budding hopes with blossoms bright
Dispel the shadowy clouds of night.

GENTLE WORDS.

Gentle words are precious jewels
   Whose worth can ne'er be told ;
We should value them as rubies
   Set in shining frames of gold.
Ah, 'tis well, like running water
   Gentle words are always free—
Do not fear to use them often
   Thus rewarded you shall be.

Should you find an erring brother
   Stumbling—just about to fall—
Give your hand to help him gently,
   Or do not help at all.
For should you speak unkindly,
   You might find your words were vain;
Go, spread roses in his pathway
   And remove the thorns of pain.

Should his feeble footsteps tremble
   On the dark and dangerous brink;
Go and throw your arms around him,
   Do not let your brother sink.
Shield him from the cruel tempter
   'Till the tempter's power is past;
Do this seven times and seventy—
   You may win his soul at last.

There is an Eye above us
   Notes the sparrows when they fall,
And with loving arms extended
   He is watching over all.
And our deeds shall not be hidden
   While our thoughts are understood;
And our acts shall be remembered—
   Both the evil and the good.

LITTLE MARY.

[A little girl whose mother was a friend of the author, said one day:
"Mother, I want to see Jesus. Please brush the clouds away."]

"I want to see Jesus;
   Mother, brush the clouds away;"
'Twas thus said little Mary
   One pleasant summer day;

And o'er her childish features
  Fell a flood of golden light,
While good angels gathered 'round her
  In their robes of fairy white.

"I want to see Jesus,
  Does He dwell among the stars
Where the amber sunlight lingers
  In mellow golden bars?
Mother, I want to see him—
  Oh! will he be my friend,
And, if I always love Him,
  Will He save me in the end?"

Years have passed, and little Mary
  In life's cares has borne a part,
And the image of the Master
  Is reflected in her heart;
And though clouds have often hidden
  Life's brightness from her view,
She has learned to always love Him
  And through faith to trust Him too.

Ah, many, very many,
  Have breathed the self-same prayer,
When their path has been surrounded
  By anguish and despair;
But Jesus kindly whispers
  He will brush the clouds away,
And welcome all who love Him
  To the realms of endless day.

WHERE SHALL THE SOUL FIND REST.

Where shall the troubled soul find rest—
  On Chimborazo's rugged steep;
Or on the Ganges' sluggish tide
  Where deadly night-winds softly creep.

Or where the frightened Arab flies
  Before the simoon's poisonous breath;
Upon the torrid, burning sands;
  No. There to linger would be death.

Deep down in hidden ocean caves,
  While all around dark billows roar;
Or where the restless, sleepless Nile
  Is washing Egypt's fertile shore.

Or out upon green Oman's sea
  Where pearls in silent beauty sleep,
And the pale moon shines languidly
  While stars their quiet vigil keep.

In lands where glittering iceberg's spire
  Points to the gloomy arctic sky;
Or mid Stromboli's crimson flame
  Shall the o'erburdened spirit fly.

Where Lebanon's tall cedars wave
  And Zion's daughters sorrowing weep;
Or out upon the emerald plains
  Where faithful shepherds watch their sheep.

Where California's golden sands
  Produce the burnished shining ores;
Or where the thundering cataract
  Its volume of destruction pours.

Ah no; beyond the Heavenly hills
  Where faith can see the immortal shore—
Our aching hearts may seek for rest,
  Where toil and sorrow come no more.

TO AN OLD FRIEND.

[The *Saturday Evening Post* was a valued literary friend of the author in childhood, and subsequently she became a contributor for its columns.]

My dear old friend your smiling face
  Reminds me of my childhood hours,
When in my heart you found a place,
  Enwreathed in fancy's budding flowers;
I loved you then, I love you still—
  As other hearts can surely say—
These memories bright my senses thrill
  And bear me back to childhood's day.

When first we met my hair was gold
    As rippling wavelets of the sea,
But now they say I'm growing old—
    I wonder, friend, if this can be?
The fields were red with clover bloom
    And gay the thrushes' woodland song,
The air was rich with sweet perfume,
    The meadow brooklet danced along.

But ah, alas, in later years,
    Where grapes 'mid clustering foliage fell,
I found the recompense of tears
    For work that seemed to me was well.
And roses gathered all too soon
    Dropped at my feet in frail decay,
While ships I hoped to greet at noon
    Would drift from out my sight away.

Dear friend, since you have older grown
    And marked the cycles of the years,
Pray tell me where the years have flown
    And where the smiles and where the tears;
Where are the friends whose rythmic flow
    Through your bright pages spoke to me;
My dear old friends of long ago—
    Oh, tell me where those friends can be?

As now I read your pages through
    With earnest thought from day to day,

You give me hope and bring to view
   For future life a brighter way.
Your heart is young, your life is old,
   In unison we thus agree,
And joys our lives have often told
   Give life to you and strength to me.

www.ingramcontent.com/pod-product-compliance
Lightning Source LLC
Chambersburg PA
CBHW030243170426
43202CB00009B/604